ONCE MORE, WITH FEELING

Once More, With Feeling

A comedy by **Harry Kurnitz**

Random House, New York

FIRST PRINTING

Library of Congress Catalog Card Number: 59-7143

Photographs by courtesy of Friedman-Abeles

Manufactured in the United States of America

ONCE MORE, WITH FEELING *was first presented by Martin Gabel and Henry Margolis at the National Theatre, New York City, on October 21, 1958, with the following cast:*

(In order of appearance)

CHESTER STAMM	Paul E. Richards
MAXWELL ARCHER	Walter Matthau
VICTOR FABIAN	Joseph Cotten
GENDEL	Leon Belasco
LUIGI BARDINI	Rex Williams
MR. WILBUR	Ralph Bunker
DOLLY FABIAN	Arlene Francis
RICHARD HILLIARD	Frank Milan
INTERVIEWER	Dan Frazer

Directed by George Axelrod
Settings and lighting by George Jenkins
Men's clothes by Michael Travis
Costumes for Miss Francis created by Scaasi

ACT ONE

Scene 1. The dressing room off the stage in a concert hall in Sioux City, Iowa. The time is the present.

Scene 2. The living room of Victor Fabian's hotel suite in Chicago. Several weeks later.

ACT TWO

Scene 1. The living room. The next afternoon.

Scene 2. The living room. Later that night.

ACT THREE

Fabian's dressing suite backstage at the Civic Auditorium. Saturday night.

ACT ONE

ACT ONE

Scene 1

The star's dressing room in the largest auditorium in Sioux City, Iowa. It is a shabby chamber, furnished with the bare minimum of lighted makeup mirror, straight chairs, a curtained alcove. On a shelf above the alcove is a moody bust of Ludwig van Beethoven. He looks out of place.

There are two doors, one at stage right, leading to the stage of the auditorium; the other, at upper stage left, apparently is the regular entrance and exit.

At rise, CHESTER STAMM *is standing in the open doorway at stage right, in an attitude of considerable tension.* CHESTER *is quite young, vaguely artistic, as indeed an assistant conductor should be. After a moment,* CHESTER *is startled out of his vigil by the entrance, at left, of* MAXWELL ARCHER, *of Maxwell Archer, Incorporated, a man of about fifty, quite well dressed. He is an impresario and the calling has left marks on him in the form of nervous movements and associated twitches.* ARCHER *crosses to join* CHESTER *in the open doorway, which makes two nervous bystanders.*

ARCHER Has he started rehearsing?

CHESTER Yes.

ARCHER How long ago?

CHESTER Twenty minutes.

ARCHER What is he doing?

CHESTER Beethoven *Fifth Symphony.*

ARCHER How far has he gotten with it?
(CHESTER, *about to speak, hears the two taps of the conductorial baton offstage, holds his finger to his lips for silence. Then we hear the opening four chords, hammered to a stop by the baton*)

ARCHER (*Extremely pained*) The first four notes? (*And as* CHESTER *nods unhappily,* ARCHER *starts pacing the shabby room*) Chester—can you hear? Is he talking to the musicians?

CHESTER Oh, yes!

ARCHER (*Alarmed*) Like that—with an exclamation mark? (CHESTER *nods again, then signals for silence.* ARCHER *leaps into the open doorway. They wait. Once more, the same four notes and the indignant rapping of the baton to drag them to a halt*) How many batons has he broken?

CHESTER Eight.

ARCHER Eight?

CHESTER And a music stand.

ARCHER Did he hit any musicians?

CHESTER Not yet.

ARCHER Did any musicians hit him?

CHESTER Not yet.

ARCHER (*Not too terribly relieved*) Well, then there is still hope. (*He stops at* CHESTER's *warning gesture; again, the same thing from the orchestra, and the stop. Then, bitterly*) Beautiful! He is supposed to be doing a Beethoven festival here. Some festival! Four notes!

(*He is pacing again*)

CHESTER Mr. Archer, what happened in Chicago?

ARCHER Chicago? Don't remind me.

CHESTER The Civic Symphony doesn't want him?

ARCHER Chester, my boy, you should only have as much money as the Civic Symphony doesn't want him.

CHESTER (*Thoughtfully*) He won't like that.

ARCHER I would like to be in an armored car when I tell him. (*And then*) Chester, for God's sake, what's happening out there?

CHESTER Sh-h-h-h . . . He's just starting again.

(*Again, the tap of the baton and the same four notes*)

ARCHER (*Suffering terribly*) Beautiful! What a magnificent interpretation! How he brings out the inner meaning of the symphony! This is how it has been everywhere. He uses symphony orchestras the way I use Kleenex.

(*Again, the tap of the baton freezes them. This time the orchestra goes past the danger mark and they react with great relief.* ARCHER *closes the door*)

CHESTER He is demanding. But he knows what he wants—he's a fine conductor.

ARCHER Sure he's a fine conductor . . . but if no orchestra will let him conduct, what good is it? I have argued, reasoned, pleaded—all that's left to try is brain surgery . . . (*And at* CHESTER'*s anxious gesture*) What is it?

CHESTER The music—didn't you notice? It stopped. (*He goes quickly to the door, opens it, looks off*) It's all right. He's only giving the orchestra a ten-minute break.

(*He takes the conductor's lush fur-collared overcoat from a hook, stands ready to drape it over him.* FABIAN *enters at right, a fine figure of a man in his middle forties, or thereabouts. The years of conducting have kept him lean and there is an air of command about him*)

FABIAN Ah, Max! Welcome to Sioux City, Iowa. (*And then, anxiously*) Well? What happened?

ARCHER (*Unhappily*) Hello, Victor . . .

FABIAN Well?

ARCHER How is the rehearsal going? Everything all right?

FABIAN What happened in Chicago, Max? . . . The Civic Symphony?

CHESTER (*Quickly*) Will you start with the Beethoven again after the break, Dr. Fabian?

FABIAN Yes, Chester. We'll tackle the slow movement this time. And tell the orchestra I want them to tackle hard. We're not just playing Beethoven—we're out to beat him. (CHESTER *goes.* FABIAN *turns on his unhappy manager*) So you fumbled it—you fumbled the Civic Symphony engagement?

ARCHER Nothing is decided yet. The trustees are meeting today and they'll call me here. (*Then, with false enthusiasm*) But don't worry—I have a fine booking lined up. The Burbank Symphony, Burbank, California. The Little Paris of the San Fernando Valley. (FABIAN *gives him a bitter look and turns his attention to his score*) Victor, do you think I like Sioux City, Iowa, or Burbank, California? If you are conducting in such places—and you are—it is because that's all we have left. In your three years as a guest conductor you have conducted every great orchestra in every great city—ONCE. New York, London, Paris, Vienna, Philadelphia, Boston—once. Are we ever invited back? Anywhere? (*And at his impatient gesture*) It's true, Victor—we are running out of orchestras—running out of cities—and soon we won't have any countries left.

FABIAN That's gratitude! My orchestra. Yes, mine. Have they forgotten in that bourgeois swamp how I slaved for eight years to make the Civic Symphony what it is today?

ARCHER Oh, no—they remember! Their decision is not musical, Victor, or artistic—simply in the interests of mental health.

FABIAN Ah! We may have had minor artistic disagreements from time to time . . . normal give and take—You exaggerate, Max.

ARCHER Exaggerate? I exaggerate? Victor, I spent years pouring oil on your troubled water. And when I couldn't do it, you had Dolly. She could tell you . . .

FABIAN Dolly? What has Dolly got to do with it? Kindly do not mention her name in my presence.

ARCHER So where should I mention it—she's your wife. (FABIAN's *back is sternly presented*) Victor—your wife—how can you hold such a grudge?

FABIAN Grudge? (*Turns on* ARCHER) The most shocking betrayal in the history of music—since Madame von Meck cut off Tchaikowsky's allowance. And you call that a grudge!

ARCHER All right, she betrayed you. Naturally when she found out that the child prodigy you were teaching privately was already twenty-six years old, a redhead, built like a Bechstein grand—

FABIAN Go on—take Dolly's side against me. You always did.

ARCHER (*A sigh of pure pleasure*) Dolly! A golden girl!

FABIAN Don't get all choked up, Max. You know what she was—a shabby little frump dragging her harp up and down Michigan Avenue, and out of pure charity I gave her a job playing with me in the Midway Movie Theatre. What a harpist! Night after night I had to take her home for private rehearsals!

ARCHER Sure, the harpist and the conductor. It's a basic law in music.

FABIAN I took this untutored peasant and sheltered her in the dignity of my art and my name. And how was I rewarded? She broke up our beautiful home.

ARCHER She had help, Victor—from you and your child prodigy pianist.

FABIAN Nonsense. Did I ever intrude in her personal life? Always lunching with the orchestra trustees, giving teas for the goddamn ladies' committees, soft-soaping contributors to the annual deficit.

ARCHER Sure. She did all that. And that's why you lasted eight years with one orchestra. And since she stopped doing it, not even eight days. (*As if transmitting a rosy vision*) Say, even yesterday, if I could have told the trustees that you and Dolly were together . . .

FABIAN You mean to say you didn't?

ARCHER (*Shocked*) But—you're separated.

FABIAN We can be reconciled, can't we? Max, get on the phone to those trustees in Chicago . . .

ARCHER Victor—wait—it takes two to make a reconciliation.

What about Dolly? . . . She's teaching in some college, isn't she?

FABIAN Yes, but out of sheer loneliness. Max, I've been too harsh with Dolly. She deserves another chance . . . (*With a snap of the fingers*) Get on the phone to the trustees.

ARCHER Victor, wait. Not so fast. The question is—will Dolly give you another chance?

FABIAN She's pining away without me . . . longing to see me. I've had three letters in the last two weeks. She pleads for another chance.

ARCHER (*Sternly*) Victor, exactly what did she say in her letters?

FABIAN Max! You ask me to reveal the intimacies of a wife's letters to her husband?

ARCHER No, certainly not. Just let me read the letters. (*The phone rings*) Maybe it's them . . . Chicago . . . (*He picks up phone*) Maxwell Archer, Incorporated. Yes, Maxwell Archer speaking. (*He covers phone. To* FABIAN) Chicago. (*Into phone*) Ah, Bardini. *Come sta?* Yes, I'm here in Fabian's dressing room. What a rehearsal! Brilliant. (*Listens*) No, you can't hear anything. He is doing a Vivaldi *concerto grosso* . . . small orchestra. (*Listens, and then dejected*) Oh? That's your final decision? (FABIAN, *with both hands, is conductorially signaling for* molto espressivo agitato, *and* ARCHER *braces himself for the attack*)

I'll tell Fabian, Bardini, but he's in such a happy mood I doubt if he cares much. Mrs. Fabian is here. (FABIAN *is beaming approval*) Yes, they are together. It's beautiful. You should see them . . . like two happy children. (*Listens*) Yes, it was sudden. But they were corresponding, and she came down here. Bardini, I wish you could see the effect on Fabian. A changed man. He was rehearsing a Mozart symphony and the clarinet player broke a reed right in the middle of the slow movement. Fabian sat down with him and personally put him in a new reed . . . (*Listens, nodding to* FABIAN; *then, as if surprised*) You want to tell the trustees? Oh? Well, sure, if you think it might change their decision. Yes, I can hold on.

(*He lowers the phone, masking the mouthpiece, exhaling heavily*)

FABIAN (*Jubilant*) What did I tell you?

ARCHER (*Covering the phone*) A decent man, with a family, how can I be such a liar?

FABIAN Max, my own orchestra, again! In a great concert hall . . . in a real city . . . with theatres, traffic jams, crime waves . . .

ARCHER But what about Dolly?

(CHESTER *enters at right*)

CHESTER Ready onstage.

FABIAN Chester, send some long-stemmed roses to Mrs. Victor Fabian, Grantly College, Grantly, Illinois. Put on the card—

(*Pauses*) . . . the first two bars of Ravel's *Introduction and Allegro* . . . (*Aside to* ARCHER) She'll like that—it's a big harp solo. (*To* CHESTER) No signature—just *"con amore."*

CHESTER How many roses?

FABIAN Oh, eight, ten dozen. And get some for yourself—

ARCHER (*Into phone*) Yes, Bardini . . . I'm here. (*Jubilant*) They accept? (*Listening impatiently, then*) No, no, Bardini, you have nothing to worry about. Fabian is positively a changed man. May I manage a Wagnerian opera company and may I have to feed them all at my own expense if I am not telling the truth. Absolutely. I'll be back tomorrow for the contract.

(*He hangs up*)

FABIAN (*Solemnly*) Maxwell Archer, if ever I imply by word or deed that you are not the greatest living impresario, then may my right hand lose its cunning.

(*He goes.* CHESTER *looks wide-eyed*)

CHESTER *Well!* (*To* ARCHER) How did he get that glow?

ARCHER Opium. (*Sadly*) I wish he hadn't smoked all of it.

(*The music has started onstage.* CHESTER *listens, all goes well, and he closes the door*)

CHESTER *You* seem tense, Mr. Archer.

ARCHER Tense? Nonsense. Look how slowly I'm twitching. (*Importantly*) Chester, I have the honor to announce that our next engagement is Victor Fabian's triumphant return to the Civic Symphony—

CHESTER After what you said—the Civic Symphony? I never expected to see him back there.

ARCHER You and about two and a half million peace-loving citizens, Chester.

CHESTER He was a legend there.

ARCHER Yes, a legend—like "Is Hitler still alive?" You don't know what went on, Chester. A reign of terror. In his orchestra the fiddlers used smelling salts the way other violinists use rosin. But how they played! Nobody before or since got that quality from the orchestra—(*The music has stopped onstage. Neither man is aware of it at first, then they both stiffen*) Chester, do you hear something?

CHESTER I don't hear anything.

ARCHER That's what I mean. (*As* FABIAN *enters quickly at right*) Victor, what is it? What happened?

FABIAN (*Lightly*) Oh, you know musicians—what crybabies they are.

(*The one who enters then,* GRISCHA GENDEL, *is wildly distraught, not without reason, as he is holding his shattered violin in both hands*)

GENDEL (*From the heart*) Dr. Fabian!

ARCHER (*Awed*) My God! You broke his fiddle.

FABIAN It was a mercy killing.

GENDEL (*In a torrential protest*) Dr. Fabian! I am a pupil of Leopold Auer. And my violin—a genuine Guadagnini. Johann Baptiste Guadagnini. Look at it. Look at it.

(FABIAN *ignores him*)

ARCHER Victor, for God's sake, at least look at it.

GENDEL (*Inspired*) The Union! I must go to the Union!

(ARCHER *has him by the arm at once*)

ARCHER No, no. Gendel, come here. Sit down. Be calm, Gendel.

GENDEL (*Hysterically*) I'm calm. I'm calm.

ARCHER Let me see your violin. (*Takes it, examining the damage, which is extensive, as the violin has apparently recently spent some time in a cement mixer.* ARCHER, *however, is most reassuring*) It's nothing, Gendel—it's only nicked a little. (*Crosses to* FABIAN, *urgently*) Victor, do something. You heard me swear to Bardini that you were a changed man. (*And to* GENDEL) Don't worry, Gendel—Dr. Fabian will do something.

(*They all look at* FABIAN *expectantly, and he rises to the occasion*)

FABIAN (*Graciously*) Very well. Max, get him another violin. (*As he exits, pauses to reproach* GENDEL) And this time, Gendel, try to take better care of your instrument.

(*He goes*)

ARCHER (*Heartily*) There, Gendel. You see—Dr. Fabian did something. (*The two taps of the baton pull him to the doorway, and again we hear the first four chords of the Beethoven* Fifth, *then the indignant rapping of the stick, stopping the orchestra.* ARCHER *heaves a heavy sigh*) A changed man! (*And to* CHESTER) Chester, my boy, if I was the Civic Symphony, for the next few weeks I would like to be in my wife's name.

Curtain

Scene 2

The living room of Fabian's apartment in an old-fashioned Chicago apartment hotel.

It is a large room with a huge slanted window at upper stage right, giving it a studio effect. Souvenirs and objects collected in FABIAN'S *conductorial travels give it something of the atmosphere of a stall in the Flea Market, but it is a warm and livable atmosphere. At right, on a raised platform, is* FABIAN'S *beloved piano. The usual sofa and chairs are strategically placed, and near the door, at stage left, is a period buffet adapted to the function of a bar. One door at stage center leads to the master bedroom and study, and downstage left is another door, opening into a second bedroom.*

At rise, the stage is deserted, then the door at left opens and CHESTER *and* ARCHER *appear, making way for* FABIAN, *who enters between them, resplendent in the most elegant component parts of his wardrobe. He is stately and composed, bending down to pat the luxurious carpeting.*

FABIAN (*Richly*) "Dear earth, I do salute thee with my hand . . ."

ARCHER Earth? You are twenty-six floors up.

(FABIAN *gives him an annoyed look, moves past him*)

CHESTER The hotel has been very co-operative . . . they brought all your own things from storage . . .

FABIAN Yes, this is my room . . . just as I dreamed of it in the long, barren years of my exile.

(*He moves around, surveying it rather grandly*)

ARCHER There is no word from Dolly. She isn't here, she hasn't got a reservation—Chester, get on the phone to that stinking college.

(CHESTER *goes to the phone. He will put in a person-to-person call to Mrs. Victor Fabian at Grantly College, Grantly, Illinois. He will hold on.* FABIAN, *meanwhile, has moved to the masses of flowers in boxes and bunches which are stacked up*)

FABIAN Ah, so I am still remembered here . . .

ARCHER Most of them are for Dolly.

FABIAN (*Annoyed*) What is she supposed to do—lie in state.

(*He moves on to the piano, raising the lid, striking a chord*)

CHESTER (*Into phone*) Will you try that Grantly call . . . (*To* FABIAN) It's your own piano—I had it tuned yesterday.

(FABIAN, *from the platform, surveys his domain*)

FABIAN Yes, this is my room. What is a room, Max? Is it four walls . . . a floor and a ceiling . . . a cubic mass of air and space? No—more than that. Memories! Memories of love and music.

ARCHER Chester, what's happening on that call?

CHESTER They're ringing.

FABIAN (*From his reverie*) Memories of three hundred forty-seven orchestral programs, including seventy-seven world premières of new music—a decade of selfless devotion to uplifting the cultural taste and aspirations of an entire community—

ARCHER Victor, we are in big trouble—even by *our* standards. Nobody has seen Dolly, or heard from her—

FABIAN Max, at the auditorium I noticed they've put in an extra row of seats. Rip them out.

ARCHER Chester, for God's sake, jiggle the hook at least.

FABIAN And at the back of stage right I want a raised hollow platform for the string bass section. What a resonance we'll get. Max, this will be an historic engagement. Just being back in this apartment, I'm starting to feel that rare something—(*Shaping it with his hands*)—like an electric current flowing through me. Don't you feel that, Max?

ARCHER Not yet. Maybe after they shave my head and slit my trousers.

FABIAN And now, a few minutes of contemplation—serene, perfect peace before I turn to my music.

(*He exits majestically*)

ARCHER He's not only crazy—he enjoys it.

(CHESTER *suddenly gets a reaction on the phone*)

CHESTER Yes? (*Listens*) Oh. No, cancel the call. (*Hangs up*)

She's not there. They don't know where she can be reached.
(*The doorbell rings.* ARCHER *is electrified*)

ARCHER Ah-ha! (*He picks up a big bunch of flowers, at random, rushes to the door. He falls back at the entrance of* LUIGI BARDINI, *a hard-faced Latin type, rather well dressed*) Bardini! *Buongiorno! Cosa va bene!* (BARDINI *looks at him coldly and comes in*) *Cher* colleague. I saw you at the airport and I tried to catch your eye, but it was such a hustle and bustle.

BARDINI You ran like a thief. You and the Maestro both.

ARCHER (*Solemnly*) May my Russian ballet company break down from hoof and mouth disease if I am not telling the truth. Chester, when I arrived, what were my first words? (*A rhetorical question*) Oh, Luigi, this is Chester Stamm, Fabian's young assistant. This is Luigi Bardini, Chester, the manager of the Civic Symphony, one of the finest men I have known in my long life in music.

BARDINI All right, Max. Where is she?

ARCHER She? Oh, you mean Dolly? Funny, we were just talking about her, Chester and I—

BARDINI Max, you lied to me.

ARCHER May I steal Carmen Amaya from Sol Hurok, and may she come down with the gout if I lied to you. (*And then, imploringly*) Not much, anyway. Dolly Fabian is coming. Positively. At the latest, tomorrow—

BARDINI That's too bad, Max, because you and the Maestro will be out of here by then.

ARCHER Luigi! Fabian is a changed man. Isn't he, Chester?

CHESTER Absolutely.

ARCHER (*Very emotional*) So gentle . . . so tolerant and understanding . . .

BARDINI Like smashing a violin on some poor fiddler's head in his last engagement?

ARCHER (*Pained*) Oh, you know about that. Well, I admit, he had a relapse there. (*Solemnly*) "To err is human, to forgive divine." (*Then, passionately*) Bardini, if you knew the enthusiasm he has for this date. Day and night he is scheming how to make the concerts better—

(FABIAN *appears, unseen for the moment, in the open center doorway.* FABIAN *closes the door with a slight slam, and as they turn, he puts his fingers to his lips*)

FABIAN Shhh! (*At* BARDINI'S *startled look*) She's asleep. (ARCHER *groans,* FABIAN *tiptoes across the room elaborately,* BARDINI *looking at him in a pained way, then whispers*) Hello, Luigi—it's good to see you again.

BARDINI (*Loud*) Maestro, for God's sake—

FABIAN Shhhh!

ARCHER Victor, he knows.

FABIAN (*Still whispering*) He knows? (*Catches himself, and in a more normal tone*) Of course. It was a harmless little joke. (*Clapping* BARDINI *on the back*) I'm delighted to see you.

BARDINI Maestro, in just about five minutes the new chairman of the trustees will be here.

FABIAN A new chairman, eh? Well, he can't be as bad as that old horror Wilbur.

BARDINI Maestro, this *is* Mr. Wilbur. Mr. Wilbur, Junior.

FABIAN Well, don't worry about a thing. I'll handle the lad.

BARDINI Maestro, Mr. Wilbur, Junior, is maybe sixty years of age. And he is coming here for only one reason—to meet Mrs. Fabian.

ARCHER She'll be here. (*Solemnly*) May I forget an appointment with Jascha Heifetz, and keep him waiting two hours in the Russian Tea Room if I am not telling the truth. Dolly will be here.

BARDINI When?

FABIAN When! She's a woman, with all the enchanting unpredictability of her sex. (*At his most engaging*) Anyway, what does it matter—I'm here. (*There is a long pause, while he examines* BARDINI's *frozen custard of a face at this announcement. He changes his tactic*) I yield to no man in my admiration for my wife. But I must point out, Bardini, that it is I who conceive and conduct these concerts, not Dolly. Mr. Wilbur must be made to understand that.

BARDINI He understands that fine, Maestro—and on that basis he ran to the air-raid shelter when your name came up.

FABIAN Oh, he did! Well, he'll wish he'd never left the air-raid shelter when—

BARDINI Maestro, for God's sake! Mr. Wilbur is not only the chairman of the trustees, his canned-goods company picks up the tab for the entire deficit every year. Three hundred thousand dollars. So, if he gets a fixation—we won't discuss how he got it—about having Mrs. Fabian here—my job is to get her. If he was holding out for Whistler's mother, I would tip my hat and do my damndest.

FABIAN Boot-licker!

ARCHER Victor, listen to Bardini. What he is saying is true.

FABIAN All right. If I must grovel before this backwoods Lorenzo de Medici, so be it.

BARDINI In that mood, Maestro, we are all going to be unemployed before nightfall.

FABIAN Listen to me. I am Victor Fabian. Conductor by trade. I have studied music since I was four years old. Until then, I only listened—but critically. I play piano and organ and for a better understanding of my work I have studied every instrument in the orchestra, including the goddamn timpani. I know harmony, theory, *solfège,* counterpoint, composition and orchestration. All of this is fused in me, waiting to explode—(ARCHER *puts his fingers in his ears*)—it will erupt in the finest series of concerts this city has ever heard. Let Alonzo P. Wilbur, Junior, stand in the path of this mighty blast—if he dares.

BARDINI Maestro, what a Japanese suicide pilot you would have made!

FABIAN "I am the captain of my soul!"

ARCHER (*Unhappily*) I am the boy on the burning deck. (*There is a buzz.* BARDINI *glances at his watch and goes to the door.* FABIAN *moves to the curve of the piano, rather elaborately studying a small score chosen at random.* BARDINI *admits* MR. WILBUR—*rather a timid type for a canned-goods tycoon*)

BARDINI (*Very big*) Mr. Wilbur! Come right in, Mr. Wilbur.

ARCHER Yes. I'm delighted to see you, Mr. Wilbur. Bardini, a chair for Mr. Wilbur.

BARDINI Mr. Wilbur, this is Maxwell Archer, and over there —Dr. Victor Fabian.

(FABIAN *slowly puts down the score, steps down and extends his hand to* MR. WILBUR)

FABIAN I'm very happy to meet you, Mr. Wilbur. I knew your father.

WILBUR So did I.

FABIAN (*Startled, but game*) And your dear mother. I wonder, does she remember me?

WILBUR Oh, yes! She talks about you all the time—(FABIAN *beams*)—she says you shortened Dad's life.

FABIAN Mr. Wilbur! Your father died at the age of ninety-three.

WILBUR True, Dad was taken from us in his prime. (*And then*) But he was mighty fond of Mrs. Fabian. (*He looks around expectantly*) Mother said I was to meet Mrs. Fabian personally.

ARCHER You will, you will. And she's very anxious to meet you. She said so. Just before she stepped out. Didn't she?

BARDINI Yes, indeed. That's what she said.

WILBUR (*Agreeably*) Then I'll wait. (*He moves to the piano, picking up a score at random*) Oh, third *Brandenburg Concerto,* by Bach. (*He starts to hum or whistle a theme.* FABIAN, *pleased, whistles the harmony, also conducting* MR. WILBUR *with neat, vivid gestures. It looks as if they have found a great common language*) You like that?

FABIAN Yes, of course.

WILBUR Well, that's what makes horse racing.
(*Tossing the score back*)

FABIAN You don't care for Bach?

WILBUR No.

ARCHER I know how you feel—Beethoven?

WILBUR Oh, no.

ARCHER Brahms?

WILBUR Brahms? Terrible!

ARCHER Scarlatti? . . . Schumann?

WILBUR I hate them both.

ARCHER Rachmaninoff!
(*He hums until* WILBUR's *fish-eye stops him*)

FABIAN (*Studies* WILBUR *for a moment*) Is it possible, Mr. Wilbur, that you just do not care for music . . . any music?

WILBUR That's it!

FABIAN But, Mr. Wilbur . . . you are the chairman of the board of a symphony orchestra!

WILBUR It came with the pickle business.

FABIAN It came with the pickle business? (*There is a tense moment, then* FABIAN *chuckles,* WILBUR *beams and* ARCHER *smiles apprehensively*) Max, did you hear what Mr. Wilbur just said? The orchestra—*MY* orchestra—came with the pickle business. (*Looks him up and down, smiling*) Very *good,* Mr. Wilbur.

WILBUR Thank you, Dr. Fabian.

FABIAN Thank you, Mr. Wilbur. (*And then, humbly*) I'm a lucky man. In this whole wide wonderful world there is only one symphony orchestra which is an annex to a pickle factory, and the Furies—(*Indicating where they lurk, in the flies*)—my personal Furies, are giving it to me.

ARCHER (*Apprehensive*) Please, Victor—

FABIAN *This* is too much! I murdered his father . . . his mother is in love with my wife . . . he hates music . . . and I'm going out to walk bare-headed—in the rain. (*Jambs his hat down on his head with both hands*) Farewell!

(*And backs out, brandishing his cane. After a moment we hear a feminine cry of "Victor—look out," and then a crash*)

FABIAN'S VOICE (*Off*) Dolly!

(*The others are gathered in the open doorway*)

ARCHER (*Pleased*) You see, Mr. Wilbur, here is Mrs. Fabian.

WILBUR He knocked her down.

ARCHER A lovers' quarrel.

(*They step aside as* FABIAN *re-enters, carrying* DOLLY FABIAN. *As will shortly become apparent she is a very pretty, well-dressed woman, bright and attractive in every way*)

FABIAN Dolly—forgive me—I didn't see you—

DOLLY Put me down, Victor. (*He does, and after an unsteady moment, she looks up, a little dazed*) Oh, my God, it's the old apartment. Nightmare Alley.

(*She sinks back on the couch*)

ARCHER (*To* WILBUR) Delirious. Lovely, but delirious.

FABIAN I'll burn this damn stick. Even though it was presented to me after I did the Beethoven Ninth in Stockholm, in nineteen forty-seven. Remember, Dolly? (*She groans*) Poor darling—let me loosen your clothing.

DOLLY Don't you dare! (*She sits bolt upright*) Thank you—that's quite all right—it won't be necessary.

ARCHER Dolly—look who is here . . . Mr. Wilbur.

BARDINI (*Quickly*) Mr. Wilbur is the new chairman of the orchestra trustees.

DOLLY Bardini! You, too? It must be Halloween.

ARCHER Dolly, you remember Mr. Wilbur. This is his son, Mr. Wilbur.

FABIAN The son of Mr. Wilbur.

WILBUR How do you do, Mrs. Fabian. I'll tell Mother you're here—she'll be pleased.

ARCHER (*Quickly*) We should leave them alone, don't you think, Mr. Wilbur? Bardini—take Mr. Wilbur to his car. You have a car, of course, Mr. Wilbur. If not, take mine.

A fifty-nine Bentley, with New York plates. M.A. One. (*He has him at the door*) Dolly, say good-bye to Mr. Wilbur. (*To* WILBUR *again*) And tell Mother, Mrs. Fabian sends her love. (*He shakes his hand warmly*) Good-bye. It was a pleasure.

(MR. WILBUR *stops in the doorway, beaming on* DOLLY)

WILBUR You're just the way Mother remembers you, Mrs. Fabian . . . (*And then to* FABIAN, *in a darker tone of voice*) You, too, Doctor.

(*He exits.* DOLLY *is about to rise, but* FABIAN *stops her with uplifted hand and urgent, ardent speech*)

FABIAN No, stay there—don't move—I want to retain this memory of you with those flowers behind you, caught in this shaft of light—

DOLLY Thank you, Victor. (*At once*) Now why should his mother—(*Pointing to the door*)—be pleased because I'm here.

FABIAN But you're here, Dolly, and that's what matters. You look absolutely radiant. How can you dress that way on the money you get from me? You're a miracle—

DOLLY Just—one—moment. I want to find out what goes on with Mr. Wilbur and his mother.

FABIAN (*Horrified*) Dolly, what a thing to insinuate! Mr. Wilbur and his mother? No, no. I refuse to believe such a thing.

DOLLY Victor, stop it—you know what I mean. Why are they

so interested in me? (*She looks from one to the other, they look innocent and preoccupied*) Well? . . .

ARCHER (*Finally*) You see, there was this deal for Victor to come back here for three weeks as guest conductor—including the Centennial Concert—and some talk of a permanent arrangement—

DOLLY Yes—go on . . .

ARCHER Well, Dolly, you know trustees . . . how they get all kinds of crazy notions . . . and then somebody—some lunatic—gave them the idea that you and Victor were coming here together . . .

DOLLY Ah-ha!

(FABIAN *leaps into the breach*)

FABIAN Max, I'm surprised at you. Here's Dolly, just in from a tiring journey—looking marvelous though—then an accident—and you're wearing her out with all this nonsense about engagements and trustees. Dolly doesn't care about all that, do you, Dolly?

DOLLY Oh, Dolly does! Dolly is a big, grown-up girl now. Dolly can smell something devious cooking. Go on, Max. Don't pay any attention to the Hour of Charm. Dolly is listening.

ARCHER Well . . . (*At a loss*) . . . where was I?

DOLLY Some lunatic had just given the trustees the idea that Victor and I were together again.

ARCHER That's it. They got that idea in their heads, and it meant so much to them . . . You get the picture, don't you, Dolly.

DOLLY And the frame! (*Turns on* FABIAN, *reproachfully*) Oh, Victor!

FABIAN Oh, Victor? What kind of a greeting is that?

DOLLY What did you expect—a crown of laurel? You don't tell me a thing, just appear out of the fog, and . . .

(*The buzzer stops them.* ARCHER *goes to the door*)

ARCHER (*En route*) S-h-h-h-h! (*Then he opens the door. It is* MR. WILBUR *again*) Mr. Wilbur! What a pleasant surprise. Dolly—Victor—look, here is Mr. Wilbur.

DOLLY The son of Mr. Wilbur.

WILBUR (*Cheerfully*) I'll only take a minute, folks. I forgot one little thing. Your program, Doctor.

FABIAN My program?

(*Everybody but* MR. WILBUR *flinches at his tone of voice*)

WILBUR It's a piece Mother particularly likes. All our guest conductors play it for her. The "Stars and Stripes Forever." (*He doesn't understand the terrible silence into which this falls*) It's by John Philip Sousa. (*And in a further effort to be helpful he whistles the "trio" of the march*) And right there, Mother likes it if the piccolo players all stand up.

FABIAN (*Ominously*) Is that all?

ARCHER Please . . . we'll discuss the details of the program later . . . please.

FABIAN We'll discuss them now.

WILBUR All right.

FABIAN The "Stars and Stripes Forever"—whether the piccolo players are standing, sitting or dangling from ropes—is out—of—the—question. Tell Mother that, and tell her also—

DOLLY O-o-o-h!

(When MR. WILBUR *turns, drawn by this squeal, she "faints" in his arms. It is a stock-company faint, apparently an ancient dodge in the* FABIAN *household, and she carries it off with practiced ease)*

ARCHER *(Accusingly, to* WILBUR*)* My God—look what you've done.

WILBUR I—I had no idea—Mother likes it—all the guest conductors play it for her.

(Meanwhile he has deposited DOLLY *on the sofa)*

ARCHER I'm sorry, Dr. Fabian. *(*FABIAN *turns his back grandly)* I'll take you to the car, Mr. Wilbur.

WILBUR *(Gratefully)* Thank you.

(He goes out with ARCHER*)*

DOLLY *(Sitting up)* After three years, I thought I'd lost the habit. What is this insane compulsion I have to keep you from making a fool of yourself?

FABIAN (*Still steaming*) The "Stars and Stripes Forever"!

DOLLY But the chairman of the board . . . and such a little thing!

FABIAN Piccolo players standing up!

DOLLY Why not? That's how Toscanini did it. And you cheered!

FABIAN I cheered another conductor? Are you sure? (*Then he takes her in his arms*) Oh, Dolly, you're right. You always were, you always will be. Go on, Dolly, give me hell. Proper hell. It's part of the fun of having you back—

DOLLY (*Startled*) Back? Back where? Oh, no, Victor! (*He kisses her*) Victor, I came here for a serious talk.
(*Struggling to get away*)

FABIAN Be still, you little fool. How can you become a great harpist, if you don't live life to the hilt. Music comes from here—
(*Putting his hand over her heart. She breaks away*)

DOLLY (*In flight*) My God, still being chased by the conductor! (*She makes the piano*) I've given up the harp, Victor—I hardly ever touch it. (*As* FABIAN *starts after her again*) No. Stay down there. I've got to tell you something. (*Earnestly*) Whatever you've told the trustees, or the management here, I can't be part of it. I'm sorry, Victor. I'm going back to the college—at the latest, tomorrow night.

FABIAN (*Wounded*) You're leaving me?

DOLLY I've left you. Two years ago. Don't you remember?

FABIAN Yes—I remember.

DOLLY Victor, I hope you have a tremendous success . . . I know you will . . . but it will have to be without me . . . I'm sorry.

FABIAN All right, Dolly. It's been wonderful seeing you again —even for these few minutes. I've missed you. (*Wistfully*) Will you have a drink with me?

DOLLY Thanks, Victor . . . maybe I will . . . a small brandy. (*She comes down from the shelter of the piano, heading for the couch, but recent memory turns her from this, to a hassock for one*) I am shaky. Ten minutes in the old apartment and I've already fainted twice. Some days, at the school, I don't even faint once. (FABIAN *has poured a snifter of brandy to the brim and now hands it to her*) Victor, what kind of a small brandy is that?

FABIAN Oh, sorry—that's for me.
(*Gives her a small drink. She takes it*)

DOLLY To your concerts, Victor.

FABIAN Thank you. And to your career, Dolly. What's it like, teaching?

DOLLY I like it. I teach first-year harmony and theory, and the harp, of course. I hope you don't mind—I'm billed as "pupil of the renowned Victor Fabian."

FABIAN I'm honored. I envy you, Dolly. The cloistered academic life . . . the unruffled calm of a small campus . . . the profound peace . . . the vast serenity—

DOLLY It's only a college, Victor—not a convent.

FABIAN Is there a student orchestra?

DOLLY Oh, yes. It doesn't amount to much, I'm afraid.

FABIAN If I can be of any help—take them through a few rehearsals—or maybe a benefit performance?

DOLLY Oh, no, Victor—I couldn't let you do that.

FABIAN (*Gallantly*) I might as well . . . I'll have plenty of free time. (*Having succeeded in making her feel miserable, he naturally tries to cash in on it*) Oh, Dolly, skip the college. We'll shoot off rockets here together . . . we'll have the town at our feet . . . you'll be queen of the Mardi Gras . . .

DOLLY I can't. (*She is truly pained*) Won't you please accept that. I'm not being coy, or hard to get— I can't.

FABIAN You've changed, Dolly. You're hard. Tell me—has someone hurt you?

DOLLY Present company included?

FABIAN Like an Iron Curtain. Damn it, you know the situation here now—they want both of us—together.

DOLLY I swear, I'd forgotten what a self-centered egomaniac

you could be. You need a wife for three weeks so you just turn down the bed and snap your fingers for good old Dolly. Take her out of the freezer, buy her a new dress and prop her up in the living room to impress the trustees. She's good in the part, and she's cheap, and she's handy.

FABIAN But you've been writing to me, Dolly. You were pleading for a chance to meet again—to talk to me—

DOLLY About a divorce! I'm sorry, Victor.

(FABIAN *turns away angrily, picks up his drink and gulps it while* DOLLY *stands by uncomfortably. Into this bleak and silent tableau comes* ARCHER, *returning*)

ARCHER (*Cheerily*) Well, how's the lovebirds?

FABIAN Divorce! Max, did you ever hear of anything like that? Go on, get a divorce. Max, fix it up for her. Whatever she wants. Get it over with. All right—you've got it—it's done. Now go on back to your veterinary college, or whatever the hell it is.

ARCHER Victor, no. If she leaves, that ends the engagement here.

FABIAN Shut up, Max. (*And to* DOLLY) Still here? What are you waiting for?

ARCHER Dolly, we'll talk. You and I. After all, you are married already all these years . . . climbing the ladder of life together, hand in hand—

(FABIAN *turns back to them, apparently revived by some idea, more his old self*)

DOLLY Victor, you know—you must know—that if it were possible to do what you ask I would do it. But it's not. You see, there's someone else now.

FABIAN I sensed it . . . a husband's intuition . . . (*Sadly*) Oh, well, it's human nature, I suppose. I turn my back—

DOLLY Turn your back? You put your foot through my harp and vanished for three years.

FABIAN I won't reproach you, Dolly. How does Shakespeare say it—"Judge not, lest ye be judged . . ."

DOLLY (*Furiously*) It's not Shakespeare—it's the Bible.

FABIAN (*With upraised hand*) Please, Dolly—let's not drag religion into this sordid story.

DOLLY Victor, you're your old self—and that's the worst thing I've ever said about anybody.

FABIAN All right, Dolly. Let's talk it over. Calmly, unemotionally, like rational people.

DOLLY Us? Rational people?
(*But she returns his smile a little at a time*)

FABIAN (*Friendly, casual*) Who's the man, Dolly?

DOLLY He's the president.

ARCHER The President!
(*It looks for a moment as if he may jump up and salute*)

DOLLY The president of the college. (*And then, to both of them*) You see why it would be awkward to live here for three weeks . . .

ARCHER Why is it awkward? You are Mrs. Fabian, not Mrs. President.

DOLLY I'm going to be. (*She looks at* VICTOR. *This is a fresh blow, but he rolls with it, nodding soberly*) His name is Hilliard. Richard Hilliard. He's a physicist. Quite a distinguished one. Doctor Hilliard. Like you, Victor. Only he has two degrees—doctor of philosophy, and doctor of science.

ARCHER Why not? The president of the college. He can hand out degrees like Hershey bars.

FABIAN Be quiet, Max. (*And to* DOLLY) I'm very happy for you, Dolly. When is the wedding day?

DOLLY Well—(*A shade uneasily for the first time*)—I more or less wanted to talk to you about it first, Victor.

FABIAN That's very thoughtful of you, Dolly, but I beg you, don't stop to consider me at all. Your happiness is what counts, Dolly. You go right ahead—make your plans—bless you.

ARCHER Just don't rush. You're not divorced.

DOLLY Max, I want to talk to Victor—alone.

ARCHER Sure.
(He starts to go)

FABIAN Sit down, Max . . . A divorce, eh? *(He sighs, in a descending scale)* Well, it isn't pleasant for a man to contemplate the shattered pieces of his emotional life—*(Amiably, to* DOLLY*)*—not that you're a shattered piece, my dear—*(Quickly, before she can swing on him)* Now, let's see about the divorce. I'm entirely agreeable. Certain steps will have to be taken, of course. For example, Step Number One, we'll have to get married. *(*DOLLY *winces, and* ARCHER *reacts mildly, not quite getting it.* FABIAN *goes on imperturbably)* The trouble is, Dolly, I don't think you'd make me a very good wife. You've developed a selfish streak, you're unco-operative, hostile—

ARCHER Stop! *(It has hit him and he is electrified)* What are you talking about? What is this about getting married?

DOLLY *(To* FABIAN*)* Blabbermouth.

ARCHER My God, you never got married?

FABIAN She wanted to be sure. *(And to* DOLLY*)* You were right, sweetheart; it didn't work out.

ARCHER All these years—and you're not married?

DOLLY Will you stop parroting that?

ARCHER *(Dazed)* Not married—it must be twelve years! Dolly, is it true?

DOLLY Yes, it's true.

(ARCHER *sits down abruptly*)

FABIAN Mark you, I wanted to marry her. Despite the gulf between us artistically and socially—

ARCHER Stop it, Victor.

DOLLY It didn't seem to matter so much then . . . Victor was conducting in the theatre—I was the harpist—and, well, I did want to be sure.

ARCHER All right. The conductor and the harpist. That's natural. But afterwards, all those years—

FABIAN Memories, memories!

DOLLY Well, Victor started getting guest engagements with symphony orchestras, and then, out of a clear sky, he was appointed permanent conductor here.

FABIAN (*Proudly*) The youngest musical director of any major symphony orchestra in the United States.

ARCHER Please, Victor, not now.

FABIAN (*Hurt*) Well, if you'd rather listen to her sleazy reminiscences.

ARCHER (*To* DOLLY) So he was conductor here. It's not a twenty-four-hour job. Couldn't you take a minute to get married?

DOLLY We were afraid to risk it. By now everyone thought we were married.

ARCHER Well, so now you're single. A technicality, but you're single. Is your fiancé such a boy scout that you can't tell him that you and Victor—(*Gropes for the right words*)—had a flirtation?

DOLLY Certainly not. But he's the president of a college. He has trustees, too. How will it look to them?

ARCHER He tells them everything?

DOLLY Max, listen: when I go to get the license, what do I tell them? That I've been single all these years? And if I say I'm divorced, I've got to have proof of it.

ARCHER (*It dawns on him*) Ah—*ha!*

FABIAN (*Warmly, generously*) Say, you have got a problem...

DOLLY (*Bitterly*) Thanks.

ARCHER No two ways about it—you need a divorce.

DOLLY You see that, don't you, Max?

ARCHER Sure, I see it . . . you see it . . . and your fiancé, he probably sees it, too. Only—(*Indicating* FABIAN)—what about him?

FABIAN (*Unctuously*) I have frequently been asked for my views on the problem of divorce and my reply has been quote I stand foursquare on the sanctity of the American home.

DOLLY I'll say one thing for you, Victor. Failure hasn't changed you—you're still awful.

FABIAN Why, you butter-fingered balalaika player!

ARCHER The way you talk to each other—you're sure you're not married?

FABIAN We were just good friends.

DOLLY You and who else?

ARCHER Children, stop it. (*They go to neutral corners*) Let's talk this out, quietly. After all, you need each other. Dolly, you want to get married and you can't because to get married you need a divorce, and you can't get a divorce because you're not married. Right?

DOLLY Right. Horrible, but right!

ARCHER All right—so you'll get married. Quietly, secretly, such things can be arranged. Then, after a short period, an amiable divorce. Dolly? Victor? What do you say?

DOLLY Fine. That's all I want.

FABIAN Well, I don't know . . . (*He is coy and shy*) Marriage is a big step. Shouldn't we have a period of getting to know each other? (*As* DOLLY *looks at him ominously*) Well, this time I want to be sure.

DOLLY What did you have in mind, Maestro—a period of about three weeks?

FABIAN Yes, three weeks would do it . . .

DOLLY Yes, lovely. What about my fiancé? What do I tell him? Just that I'm moving in with you again?

FABIAN He might be one of those absent-minded professors: wouldn't even notice.

ARCHER We could explain. Tell him something—(*Proudly*) I am a terrific liar.

DOLLY Victor, please. I am appealing to you—

FABIAN (*Suddenly*) My God! My rehearsal! (*Flexing his fingers*) Remember the first time I rehearsed this orchestra, Dolly? I stayed up all night drinking black coffee and studying my scores; finally I was so nervous the baton was flying out of my fingers. And you were pacing the floor beside me, worrying about your new dress—was it too tight, or too low, or too little or too late?—Remember, Dolly?

DOLLY Victor, I love strolling down Memory Lane with you. But not now. What about my problem?

FABIAN Sure, sure. We'll meet later for a cocktail and talk it all out.

DOLLY We can talk it all out right now.

FABIAN And be late for my rehearsal?

DOLLY Just say yes. Or if that takes too long, simply nod your head (*As he smiles appreciatively, moving past her*) Please, Victor.

(*He turns, gives her a long, steady, reproachful look*)

FABIAN Dolly, what has this cow-country college done to you? You left me a brilliant, sparkling, spirited woman—and you've come back as the sniveling heroine of some soap opera. (*Patting her shoulder affectionately, smiling*) But don't worry—we'll change all that. (*As if it were a great boon*) You'll be your old self, never fear.

DOLLY My old self? Is that your best offer?

FABIAN You were wonderful, Dolly.

DOLLY I was awful. Conniving and scheming, lying and soft-soaping. Why? For the holy cause of Victor Fabian. Every day, every hour, every minute, so you could have your own selfish way.

(FABIAN, *surprisingly enough, is beaming with pleasure at this recital*)

FABIAN Right. And how you must have loved it— How else could you have been so good at it? Even today, when the "Stars and Stripes Forever" loomed up, you picked up your cue just on sheer instinct. You loved hoodwinking old Mr. Wilbur, and I'm counting on you to give Mother the same razzle-dazzle. We're two of a kind, Dolly. The courts may dissolve a union between a man and a woman, but no power this side of the Pearly Gate separates a conductor and a harpist. (*Then, abruptly*) Now that's enough distraction. I have only a few minutes to compose myself for my rehearsal. And this is the one that counts. Max, my music.

ARCHER Here.

(He hands him the case)

FABIAN *Thanks.* (*To* DOLLY) My coat, please. (*She moves rather mechanically, as if absorbed, taking it from the chair and coming back to him with it*) Just over my shoulders, please.

(He turns and she is about to drape it there, and then the spell snaps)

DOLLY NO!!! (*She throws the coat violently on the floor*) There's your coat, you road-company Svengali! (*She stamps on it, as* FABIAN *winces*) My God, I nearly stepped right back into that trap. (*Mimicking him*) Max, my music. Dolly, my coat. My rehearsal, my career. Take them, Maestro—they're all yours. You can count me out. If you can count. In any tempo from *adagio con moto* to *presto agitato.*

(*She goes, slamming the door.* ARCHER *winces, but despite the vehemence of her exit* FABIAN *stands looking at the door thoughtfully, calmly*)

FABIAN Pity . . . I nearly had her there . . . (*Sadly, with resignation*) Well, I hate to do this, but she's asking for it. Get hold of her president, Max, that Dr. Hilliard.

ARCHER Victor, is that fair?

FABIAN Of course not. Get on the phone; get him down here.

(*He picks up his coat, shakes it out tenderly, smoothing the fur collar down with a loving hand.* ARCHER, *at the phone, is hesitant*)

ARCHER Victor, do you think we should?

FABIAN (*Calmly*) We owe it to him. (*He starts out*) He ought to be here—his romance is on the rocks.

(FABIAN *goes out*)

Curtain

ACT TWO

ACT TWO

Scene 1

The living room, the next afternoon.

At rise, CHESTER *is arranging a large group of framed autographed photographs of celebrities, musical and civilian, placing them in some prescribed order on the mantel at upper stage center. He is apparently puzzled by the disposition of one item, and while he is pondering it,* MAXWELL ARCHER, INCORPORATED, *enters at left.* ARCHER *is a man at peace, floating on a cloud, humming Beethoven's* Seventh Symphony, *first movement, through his cigar.*

CHESTER Hello, Mr. Archer.

ARCHER Ah, there, Chester, my boy.

CHESTER Excuse me—does Eugene Ormandy go in front of Rudolf Serkin, or in back?

ARCHER In back, Chester. Living conductors, always in back—soloists, minor composers and movie stars in the middle—child prodigies in the bathroom.

(*He is humming a happy fragment of something*)

CHESTER Rehearsal, I take it, went well?

ARCHER Like silk. Like sailing in tropical waters. One hour

of rehearsing difficult music and Fabian did not break one single baton.

CHESTER Fabian?

ARCHER *Fabian.* (*Wistfully*) If only he would be reasonable about that lousy march. Did you do what I told you, Chester, about the music?

CHESTER I tried. I slipped the "Stars and Stripes Forever" into his case, but he found it and tore it to shreds.

ARCHER How do you like that? A piece that Toscanini was proud to play.

CHESTER Can't we find something else? Is that all Mr. Wilbur's mother likes?—Sousa marches?

ARCHER That's it. The old lady must be a retired drummer.

(*The buzzer sounds.* CHESTER *goes to the door, admitting* DOLLY)

DOLLY Hello, Chester. Anybody home?

ARCHER I'm here, I'm here. Come in, Dolly, my dearest Dolly.

DOLLY Hello, Max.

ARCHER (*Looking her over*) Marvelous! Like a young harpist coming to her first engagement.

DOLLY Perish the thought!

CHESTER Excuse me. Some new orchestra parts have come in and I want to check them for tomorrow's rehearsal.

ARCHER Fine. Go ahead, Chester. (CHESTER *exits at center*) Nice boy. Gifted, too. He'll make a fine conductor one of these days.

DOLLY Well, he's young. Who knows—in his lifetime, they may discover a cure for it. (*And then*) Victor not back yet?

ARCHER Late rehearsal, but he won't be long. And what a rehearsal! Want to drop over, hear a little?

DOLLY No, thanks. I've had enough rehearsals—and performances.

ARCHER Dolly! That's from hanging out with the college crowd—(*Packs a load of contempt into the word*) Civilians! But you, you're a musician. You're not even teaching—God forbid!—algebra, or something like that. You're teaching music.

DOLLY Yes, but I'm not living and breathing and smelling it twenty-four hours a day. I leave that to you and Victor now. I am a civilian, Max. And you know something—I listen to music for pleasure these days.

ARCHER (*Startled*) Music? For pleasure? (*Skeptically—still doubtful*) Music for pleasure! Could be . . . I never thought of it that way. You really don't miss it, Dolly? . . . The concerts? . . . The excitement?

DOLLY No, Max. Truly. Not a bit.

ARCHER But you studied, and played . . . for years.

DOLLY With me, I don't think it was habit-forming. I know it is with some musicians. They stay away from it for years even and then one whiff of rosin and they've got that old chromatic feeling again. My father was like that. A trombone player—and not bad for a man with short arms—(*Illustrating what Dad's trouble would be like*) During the depression he couldn't get work as a musician, so he went into the insurance business. He did well and didn't touch the trombone for years. Then one day he passed a Salvation Army band playing hymns on a street corner and the trombone player had a solo in "Jesus Wants Me for a Sunbeam." He listened, then went straight to the Union, paid up his dues and went on the road as a sideman with Buck Tremain's Varsity Eight. And Pop was nearly sixty.

ARCHER Beautiful! A true music lover.

DOLLY I'm a music lover, Max. But for me, from now on, just music on records. (*With a sigh*) If parents only knew what they were starting when they give their children music lessons.

ARCHER All right—so you escaped from all this. You're a civilian, you'll marry a civilian—who knows, you'll have civilian babies. Does that mean you hate Victor?

DOLLY (*Slowly*) No, I don't hate him. I never did. And there was a time when I loved him—very much. Not as much as he loves himself—for that kind of romance you have to go clear back to *Tristan and Isolde.*

ARCHER He's changed, Dolly. You should have seen him at rehearsal yesterday, and today—

DOLLY Max, I am not moving in here again. I should have gone back to the college yesterday; I must leave tonight, or tomorrow morning. I want to talk to Victor again . . .

ARCHER The whole city is clamoring for you. Look—new flowers came today. They love you here, Dolly. The trustees, the subscribers, the ladies' committee—everybody.

DOLLY And I love them. But I do not love Victor Fabian.

ARCHER Who's asking you to love him? Just live with him for three weeks. I am going to help you—we have a plan.

DOLLY Max, please, I'm in enough trouble.

ARCHER May I book a benefit for the D.A.R. and may I make a mistake and send them Paul Robeson, if I'm not telling the truth. Listen—don't talk, just listen—(*Conspiratorially*) Bardini already has a marriage license—so secret the Mayor doesn't even know about it. Also, a judge is standing by. You are married, Victor makes a triumphant comeback, and one-two-three you are in Acapulco, where my own cousin, Don Felipe Archer, the finest divorce lawyer south of the Rio Grande, meets you at the plane—(*Triumphantly*) It is all arranged with Bardini—Victor—everybody. Just say the word, and, this afternoon, you are a bride and practically a divorcée— Well?

DOLLY Max, that's glorious—but impossible.

ARCHER All right. What's your solution?

DOLLY I don't know. I was hoping Victor would be reasonable.

ARCHER Victor—reasonable? That changed he is not. (*Wistfully*) Dolly, you think maybe if you explained things to your fiancé—the president . . . ?

DOLLY Tell him I have to move in here with Fabian?

ARCHER You think he would mind?

DOLLY Wouldn't you?

ARCHER I don't know. I'm so used to doing crazy things for musicians. (*The buzzer at the door is heard.* ARCHER *answers it, admitting* BARDINI *in all his accustomed agitation*) Ah, Luigi—come in. Dolly is here.

DOLLY Just leaving.

BARDINI No—wait! (*She stops*) Max, where did you go? Why did you leave the rehearsal?

ARCHER Some private business. But they didn't need me. It was going beautifully. I was just telling Dolly how beautifully it went, wasn't I? (*Something in* BARDINI's *manner communicates itself*) It—it didn't go beautifully?

BARDINI (*Distinctly*) Two minutes after you left, Fabian tore the shirt right off a musician's back.

ARCHER (*Explosively*) No!

BARDINI No? (*He whips out part of a shirt, almost the whole sleeve, waves it*) Here. I'm sorry I couldn't get the part that was monogrammed. This came off the leader of the second violin section, the orchestra representative on the board of directors, and a vice-president of the Union.

ARCHER (*Shuddering*) No!

(*He gropes for some brandy, pours some, and passes the bottle to* BARDINI, *who drinks from the bottle*)

BARDINI It was going beautifully . . . Then in *La Mer,* he had the strings play stand by stand, then individually, and suddenly batons were snapping and the next thing I knew—this—

(*Waving the shirt again*)

DOLLY Blind and destructive as it is, you've got to admire that ego.

ARCHER You admire it—it makes me sick. (*To* BARDINI) Luigi, get this fiddle player up here—what's his name?

BARDINI Gendel. Jascha Gendel.

ARCHER Gendel? (*He utters something like a death rattle*) Oh, my God, on our last engagement Victor smashed his brother's violin.

BARDINI (*Fervently*) Miss Dolly, we need you now. If I could count on you to talk to this musician—

ARCHER (*Pleading*) Dolly, *yes.*

DOLLY Max, *no.*

ARCHER Bardini, get over to the Union and stop this fiddle player from making a stink. Get him up here. I'll talk to him.

BARDINI I'll try.

(*He starts out dolefully, leaving the shirt remnant behind*)

ARCHER Not like that. With spirit, and determination.

BARDINI (*Weakly*) Sure, Max.

(*He goes out at left*)

DOLLY He's really changed. He's worse.

ARCHER (*Pacing*) I am not giving in. I am not a Hollywood agent with antique furniture and a bedside manner. My God, what I have done for my clients. I have risked my life. Yes, I, Maxwell Archer, Incorporated, in Odessa, when I smuggled out my great Russian tenor, Valentinoff, disguised as a wagonload of smoked fish. It was a sensational scandal. The Bolsheviki put a price on my head.

DOLLY Well, good luck with everything, Max. If it would do any good, I would help, but you've got to face the facts: Victor Fabian is a certifiable psychopath, with maniac overtones, in a downhill phase.

(*Among those privileged to hear this summation is* VICTOR FABIAN, *who looms up in the doorway at left. His coat is slung over his shoulders, his head is neither bloody nor bowed*)

FABIAN (*To* DOLLY) Ah, it's Broken Blossoms.

DOLLY (*Pleasantly*) Hello, Victor. I was just saying to Max what a monster you were.

FABIAN That's what the ignorant peasants called Galileo.

(ARCHER, *incapable of speech, is waving the remnant of shirt.* FABIAN, *having shed his coat, looks at it with distaste*)

ARCHER Victor, what have you done?

(FABIAN *peers at the torn bit of shirt*)

DOLLY He doesn't recognize it since you took off the violinist.

FABIAN Oh, that. (*And as* ARCHER *continues to wave the shirt in his face*) Well, don't act as if it were the Twilight of the Gods. So I abused a violinist. One violinist. That's what they're for. Why do you think God made fiddle players?

ARCHER He made this one a member of the board of directors.

DOLLY And a vice-president of the Union.

ARCHER (*A broken man*) Why, Victor—just one word—*why?*

I heard nearly the whole rehearsal. I walked away on a cloud. It was milk and honey. And now—(*He crushes the torn bit of shirt*) This.

FABIAN It was a terrible rehearsal. Nearly as bad as yesterday's. (*And as* ARCHER *is about to protest*) No, don't tell me how smooth and jolly it all went. I know they loved the conductor and everyone was having a fine time, but we were miles away from a performance. This fellow—(*Pointing to the remnant of the shirt*)—he was the worst. He was *smiling*. Do you hear, smiling! How dare he enjoy himself in my orchestra? Well, I tore the smiles off all of them along with his shirt. You should have heard the rest of the rehearsal. They were tense, frightened, they sat up straight on the edge of their chairs, hating me—but they played.

ARCHER So instead of a baton, conduct with a flame thrower. That way, you'll really get results.

FABIAN Max, no orchestra gives me anything. Never. I have to fight them for it. I am not a legendary Italian, or a former Nazi. I am an American conductor, born and trained right here. I came up the hard way—on the elevator pit of a movie theatre, with the same Union card as the orchestra musicians. To them that's a license to sit back comfortably in their chairs and give me as much as they think I ought to have. I'm one of them, and on that basis they would relax and destroy me. (*Then, with a smile*) Fortunately, however, I am a monster. Oh, I may have gone too far with this one particular man—but Dolly can handle that.

DOLLY (*Startled*) Dolly? (*Looks around*) Dolly who? (FABIAN *tosses her the fragment of shirt*) Oh, no. None of that.

(*She tosses it right back to him*)

FABIAN Keep it, Dolly. (*Throwing it back*) Don't you see, it's a talisman for our wedding—something borrowed and something blue. (*As she stares at him*) Max, didn't you tell Dolly about our surprise?

ARCHER I told her, I told her.

FABIAN "Happy the bride the sun shines on today." It's all arranged, Dolly. License, judge . . . the works . . . just what you wanted.

DOLLY Yes, Victor. But I am not moving in here again for three weeks. (*Pleading*) Victor, how can I? You know my circumstances.

FABIAN (*Ardently*) To hell with circumstances. It's spring, Dolly—or it will be in a few months—"the voice of the turtle is heard in our land . . ."

ARCHER Wait . . . children—quiet, everybody. (*Importantly*) Dolly, what if you stayed only until after Victor's first concert? Three days only. Victor, what do you say?

FABIAN (*Gallantly*) Anything. A minute . . . an hour . . . a day, a month, a year—

DOLLY I'll take a minute. (*She is tempted, though*) Max, do you mean that? You'll really let me go after the concert Saturday night?

ARCHER May I sit through an uncut performance of *Parsifal* without a bite to eat if I'm not telling the truth . . . Absolutely. Sunday morning you are back in college—married, and practically divorced.

DOLLY (*Speculating*) Three nights? (*She looks at* FABIAN *searchingly*) Victor, you realize that this marriage would be in name only?

FABIAN (*With nobility*) I have my books... and my music...

ARCHER Come on. Bardini has the judge waiting only till three o'clock. Dolly, you heard Victor. He promised.

DOLLY Yes . . . what does he mean by that?

ARCHER What do you care what he means. You've got two bedrooms, with locks.

FABIAN (*Pained*) With locks? (*And then instantly, recovering*) Yes, of course . . . with locks. You'll be as safe as if you were in your own bed.

DOLLY (*Firmly*) And I will be.

ARCHER Where else? (DOLLY *hesitates,* ARCHER *waits impatiently,* FABIAN, *at the piano, picks out the "Wedding March"*) Come on, Dolly.

DOLLY (*Plaintive*) I've got nothing to wear!

FABIAN Dolly, you look absolutely radiant. Every inch a bride. And I say now, before God, man and my agent, that I, Victor Fabian, take you, Dorothea—

DOLLY All right, Victor. Save it for the judge. (*She looks hard at* FABIAN, *then slips her wedding ring off*) Is it *us* . . . getting married . . . like real people? (*She hands* FABIAN *the ring*) Here, Victor—you'll need this.

(FABIAN *takes the ring, holds it for a moment, then kisses* DOLLY *lightly on the cheek. He goes to the door at left, picking up his hat and coat en route.* ARCHER, *as best man and agent for the proceedings, extends his arm to* DOLLY *with a courtly bow*)

ARCHER Come, Dolly.

(*He hums the "Wedding March" as she joins him, and as they both exit, ahead of* FABIAN, *she chimes in, splendidly off-key*)

FABIAN (*Wincing*) B-flat, Dolly! Damn it, will you never learn!

(*He follows them out*)

Curtain

Scene 2

The living room, later that night.

At rise, the stage is dark, then CHESTER *enters, snaps on the light and ushers in* JASCHA GENDEL, *the most recently martyred violinist. He bears a startling resemblance to his brother* GRISCHA, *accounted for perhaps by the fact that both parts are played, for art and economy, by the same man.* JASCHA *wears a long overcoat, long muffler, and face to match.*

CHESTER Come in—please. Dr. Fabian hasn't returned, but I know he'll be back in a few minutes—(*The phone rings*) Ah—that may be word from him. (*He goes to answer it, picks up phone*) Hello. Oh, hello, Mr. Archer. I just came in. (*And then, elaborately*) With Jascha Gendel, the violinist —(*Glancing up at* JASCHA) Yes, that violinist. Fine. In a few minutes. (*Hangs up*) He's coming. Just a few minutes.

JASCHA (*Stiffly*) It is hardly necessary. I have written an account of the entire affair for the Union, and the board of directors—

CHESTER But you want Dr. Fabian's side of the story, don't you? That's the American way.

JASCHA Well—if you're sure it will be only a few minutes... (*He takes off his gloves, very deliberately, and under his gloves he has* another pair of gloves. *The second pair he removes, finger by finger. Then he sees* CHESTER *staring wide-eyed*) I could catch a chill in my finger.

CHESTER Yes, of course.

(*He helps* JASCHA *off with his coat, etc., putting the items on a chair.* JASCHA *examines the fingers of his left hand carefully, then tucks it under his jacket*)

JASCHA Thank you.

CHESTER You know, you and your brother resemble each other quite a bit.

JASCHA You think so? Grischa has a much heavier vibrato—(*Illustrating it with hand and wrist*)—and I find his bowing sometimes is a trifle coarse.

CHESTER I meant, physically. You look like each other. (*Ingratiatingly*) Would you like a drink? (*Indicating the bar setup*) Scotch . . . rye . . . champagne . . . anything at all?

JASCHA (*Politely*) Do you have some lighter fluid?

CHESTER Lighter fluid?

JASCHA For my hand-warmer.

(*Exhibiting the device, the fingers of his left hand curled around it snugly*)

CHESTER No, but I can call room service.

JASCHA It doesn't matter. (*He has moved to the piano, now glances approvingly at the framed photographs*) Ah—

Moiseivitch . . . Milstein . . . Piatigorsky . . . Solomon— (*Picks up one of the pictures, stares at it curiously*) And who is this? I can't make out the signature.

CHESTER (*Awed*) That's President Eisenhower!

JASCHA Oh! (*Gives it another glance*) Fine-looking man.

(*Puts the picture back. He sits down, quite primly, and there is a heavy silence. It doesn't bother* JASCHA, *who is off on Cloud Seven, but* CHESTER *fights against it*)

CHESTER (*After a few false starts*) You know, we—that is, Dr. Fabian and I—met your brother in our last engagement.

JASCHA I know. I saw the X-ray pictures.

CHESTER He wasn't hurt. And he has a new violin.

JASCHA He has a new violin. But he also has the old psychiatrist. He is a laughingstock in the orchestra. He is having a nervous breakdown. Now his vibrato is really heavy. (*Demonstrating with his hand and wrist, then adding pleasantly*) But it is all written out in my report.

(*He exhibits a bulky envelope, at the sight of which* CHESTER *shrinks a bit, then he puts it back in his pocket and the rest is silence*)

CHESTER (*Forcing it, after a moment*) What do you think of the situation in France nowadays?

JASCHA (*Agreeably*) French woodwinds play quite well; I don't care for the string tone.

CHESTER I was thinking of their Colonial problem.

JASCHA Ah, yes, the Colonial. (*It strikes a chord*) When I was in the Boston Symphony a boiler blew up in Symphony Hall and for two weeks we played our concerts in the Colonial Theatre. Our problem was with the stage.

CHESTER (*Desperately*) The French problem is in North Africa.

JASCHA (*Suspiciously*) North Africa? What is the Boston Symphony doing in North Africa.

CHESTER (*Helplessly*) They got confused.

(*He is enchanted by the sound of the buzzer, and jumps up to answer it.* ARCHER *comes in, full of cordiality, followed by* DOLLY. JASCHA *rises, looking about warily*)

ARCHER Ah, here is our young artist. Dolly, look, here is concertmaster Jascha Gendel.

DOLLY How do you do.

JASCHA Dr. Fabian is not here?

ARCHER He is delayed. Just a few minutes, my dear young colleague.

JASCHA I should go home. All day long, I was so upset, I didn't practice. (*Moving the fingers of his left hand nervously*) Besides, I don't know if I should wait for Dr. Fabian— I have my report for the Union—

ARCHER Now, Jascha, we don't want the Union to mix into what is a simple artistic disagreement.

JASCHA Dr. Fabian tore the shirt off my back. While I had my coat on. And two weeks ago, he struck my brother Grischa over the head with his own violin, an Italian instrument made by Johann Baptiste Guadagnini in Cremona in seventeen hundred thirty-one. It is all written down in my report—

(ARCHER *has him by the hand, tries to get him to sit down*)

ARCHER Yes, very artistic, I'm sure, but—

DOLLY (*Comes between them suddenly*) Max! Be careful! (*She gently detaches his hand from* JASCHA's) Never grip an artist's hand in that rough, crude way— Do you want to do him an injury?

(JASCHA *looks at her suddenly the way Lassie, the collie, used to look at Freddy Bartholomew*)

JASCHA Thank you, Mrs. Fabian.

ARCHER (*No fool*) Yes . . . excuse me—(*He takes* JASCHA's *hand tenderly, carefully*) Stupid of me. (*Looks at the limp member he is holding*) Beautiful. So expressive.

(JASCHA *ignores him entirely*)

JASCHA You are very understanding, madame

ARCHER Chester, please, come—I have some very important telegrams to get out. (*And to* JASCHA) Stay a moment with Mrs. Fabian, my boy.

JASCHA (*Uncertainly*) It is late already . . .

DOLLY Just a moment. Give your hand a chance to breathe.

JASCHA Very well.

(*He lets himself be drawn to the sofa, and seated.* ARCHER *and* CHESTER, *meanwhile, have vanished at center*)

DOLLY You know Max Archer, don't you?

JASCHA Yes, of course. (*Bitterly*) He is a fine man, provided you are Jascha Heifetz or Nathan Milstein. You know something, Mrs. Fabian, I saw him once about arranging a debut. He told me to come back when I was ready for my Farewell Tour. Tonight it's different.

DOLLY He's Victor's manager. He's afraid of you because you're on the board of directors of the orchestra and an officer of the Union.

JASCHA Right. (*Surprised*) I didn't expect to hear it from you.

DOLLY Oh, I'm no part of all this . . . not any more . . . I'm a simple teacher now, at a small college.

JASCHA You teach? So do I. I'm at the Conservatory.

DOLLY The Conservatory! I didn't know they engaged such young professors.

JASCHA The truth is, I am only an assistant. But I am the

youngest. The others, the established professors, they ridiculed me.

DOLLY The way the ignorant peasants ridiculed Galileo.

JASCHA Excuse me. I am not familiar with the Italian composers.

DOLLY In the symphony, there are thirty-six violinists, yet of them all, when he lost his head, Victor picked you.

JASCHA (*Dubiously*) It was an honor?

DOLLY Yes!

JASCHA (*Groping*) He admired my shirt—was that it?

DOLLY No! He sensed something. He realized that in order to dominate the orchestra completely, he would first have to command *you.*

JASCHA Ah-ha! (*Pleased*) Yes, I see . . .

DOLLY Stemming from his basic insecurity . . .

JASCHA Do you really think Dr. Fabian is insecure? You should have seen the grip he had on my shirt.

DOLLY Insecure . . . and jealous of other men's achievements . . .

(*Patting his hand*)

JASCHA (*He's loving it*) Yes. Go on, Mrs. Fabian.

DOLLY Something in your playing undoubtedly caught his attention. A phrase, or a distinctive bowing, or some bit of style. Subconsciously, he was on the watch for something like that in the rehearsal. Victor is a tyrant. Oh, he has skill, and talent, but underneath is this stream of tyranny which forces him to break and subdue the unusual artists around him.

JASCHA Amazing (*Weakening*) Perhaps this should be in my report—in Dr. Fabian's favor?

DOLLY It won't matter. Your report, and the petition of the musicians, that should be enough for the trustees. (*And as* JASCHA *fingers the envelope*) You see, Victor and I have been separated. In this engagement we were going to attempt a reconciliation. I hoped that he had changed, but in his attack on you, I see that he has not. It won't work. (*Wistfully*) I'll have to go away again.

JASCHA (*A cry of pain*) Oh! I'm sorry! (*Her suffering hurts him and it seems to be his responsibility*) Mrs. Fabian—(*Pushing the envelope at her*) Take this!

DOLLY The report? But why?
(*Still, she takes a good grip on it*)

JASCHA I feel that we should give Dr. Fabian another chance—you and I, together. After all, only the second rehearsal—

DOLLY But after what he did?

JASCHA Temperament. And to tell you the truth, it was an old shirt.

DOLLY And after the way he treated your brother?

JASCHA Just between ourselves, sometimes I myself find the way Grischa plays quite irritating, and I am not so sure his violin is a genuine Guadagnini—

(*The buzzer at the door stops him.* ARCHER *comes back into the room and goes quickly to the door*)

ARCHER (*As he goes*) Do not disturb yourself—

(JASCHA *has risen and* ARCHER *opens the door, admitting* FABIAN. *At the sight of him,* JASCHA *instinctively puts up a hand to protect his shirt*)

DOLLY Victor, come and shake hands with Jascha. (FABIAN *approaches, his hand out, and* JASCHA *extends his own warily*) Carefully, Victor!

(*They shake hands*)

JASCHA Mrs. Fabian has made certain things clear to me. I have already forgotten what happened at the rehearsal this afternoon.

FABIAN (*Generously*) Well, I'm not one to hold a grudge.

(*He pats* JASCHA *on the back and exits at center*)

JASCHA (*Humbly*) Thank you. (*Something has happened to reverse the roles in the situation, but* JASCHA *never gets a chance to figure it out.* ARCHER *is already holding his coat and both* ARCHER *and* DOLLY *bundle him into it in a twinkling, winding the scarf around him a few times and rushing him to the door. As* JASCHA *goes, dazed—*) Good night . . . thank you . . . thank you . . .

DOLLY Good night, Jascha. Take care of your beautiful hands. (*She sees him over the threshold, then closes the door and leans against it for a moment*)

ARCHER A fantastic performance. (*Kisses her hand respectfully*) If you were the Secretary of State, all of Russia would be in Kansas tomorrow morning.

DOLLY I'm ashamed of myself.

ARCHER You? A genius? Ashamed of yourself?

DOLLY If only he hadn't been so naïve . . . such a sitting duck.

FABIAN (*As he enters from door at center*) You're right, Dolly. I know just how you feel. But I'll make it up to him. From now on, this is National Be-Kind-to-Fiddle-Players Week. (*As* CHESTER *comes in*) Chester, first thing tomorrow, get Jascha Gendel some new shirts.

CHESTER Yes, sir. How many?

FABIAN Oh, eight, ten dozen—and get some for yourself. And, Chester, don't just stand there—kiss the bride.

CHESTER May I?

(*He gives* DOLLY *a chaste salute*)

DOLLY Thank you, Chester. I wish you could have been with us. It was the kind of ceremony every girl dreams about: furtive, sneaky . . .

ARCHER It was beautiful. I cried, for the first time since I turned down a chance to manage Leonard Bernstein. (*Defensively*) He was so nice . . . talked so pleasantly . . Who knew he was a genius!

FABIAN If you hurry, Max, you might still get him.

ARCHER Yes, come, Chester, I have a mountain of telegrams to answer.

FABIAN (*Seeing him out*) You must not let me take up too much of your valuable time, Max. It isn't fair to the rest of your clients. I'm too demanding. I realize that now, and I'm turning over a new leaf. (*Emotionally*) Good night, my old friend.

ARCHER (*Stunned*) Am I in the right room? You know something, Victor, you should get married every day. Good night.

(FABIAN *closes the door, rather elaborately locks it, the click of the bolt coming through nicely. Then he pours some wine, brings the glasses to the table, starts some music on the phonograph. It is all highly seductive, except that* DOLLY *is watching him suspiciously*)

FABIAN So this is married life, eh? Well, no wonder it's so popular. (*Raising his glass*) To us, Dolly.

DOLLY (*Agreeably*) To us—(*Adding*)—wherever we are.

(*They drink, then* FABIAN *pours more wine*)

FABIAN Darling, wouldn't you like to slip into something loose?

DOLLY Yes . . . (*Then, firmly*) The elevator.

FABIAN (*Reproachfully*) Dolly!

DOLLY Victor, please try to remember one essential fact. I am engaged to another man.

FABIAN But, damn it, you're married to me.

DOLLY A marriage of convenience.

FABIAN And we're living together!

DOLLY You're living together. I'm not.

FABIAN (*Bitterly*) That certainly is convenient. (*And back to the attack*) Dolly, this icy calm isn't you. Not the real you. It's ridiculous for you to treat me like an absolute stranger. My God, I remember the mole on your—

DOLLY (*Outraged*) Victor!

FABIAN Can I help it if I remember. There it was, the cutest little mole, right on your—

DOLLY Stop it! Stop it, or I'll walk out right now. I mean it. (*And then, embarrassed*) Anyway, I had it removed.

FABIAN You had it removed? (*Wounded beyond belief*) Our mole?

DOLLY (*With dignity*) You won't achieve anything by making me self-conscious, Victor.

FABIAN You and your goddamn poise!

DOLLY I agreed to stay here because you promised we would be just good friends.

FABIAN I meant very good friends.

DOLLY Oh, no! There are separate bedrooms. With locks, as I recall, so there will be no tiptoeing about in the night. (*As* FABIAN *nods glumly*) We have to share the bath, but I expect you to behave like a gentleman.

FABIAN I'll wear a bathing suit.

(*He is sulking so profoundly that* DOLLY *shakes her head in wonder*)

DOLLY Victor, all those promises this afternoon—you didn't mean any of them, did you?

FABIAN Of course! I meant every word I said! (*Adding loftily*) I happen to have changed my mind. That's all.

DOLLY Oh, Victor! (*She laughs, and her guard is down for a moment.* FABIAN *sneaks under it, and kisses her. She is shaken a bit*) That—that was unfair.

FABIAN I enjoyed it. Remember me—selfish Victor? Anyway, I don't have your Yogi calm. Since you set foot in this room I've been disturbed and confused by a thousand memories.

DOLLY Don't you think I remember? The trouble is, I remember all of it. Your memories are of parties and triumphant tours and making love—

FABIAN You know that mine is a romantic nature.

DOLLY Now, that I do remember. And in your generous, romantic fashion, you spread it around quite a bit.

FABIAN Dolly, that is unfair. The girl *was* a prodigy. Big for her age, I grant you. (*Earnestly*) But, Dolly, she didn't mean a thing. You must have known that. If she was the reason, you were wrong, Dolly—and foolish.

DOLLY No . . . that wasn't the reason.

FABIAN Damn it, what was?

DOLLY Think, Victor . . . think back a bit. There was a great love in your life, and it wasn't me—or the child prodigy. The orchestra, and the sound it produced. (*Over his impatient gesture*) Sound. Rich, round, glorious tone. I might as well have been living with a tuning fork. You turned to me when you were in trouble, and the rest of the time . . . well, you were scaling the heights and I found myself respectfully two steps behind struggling with the heavy luggage.

FABIAN (*Solemnly*) Not one word of that is true.

DOLLY Victor—tonight—a few minutes ago! Surely you can remember that far back? Married five minutes and what was I doing? Placating a musician you man-handled. Tomorrow, bright and early, I tackle Mr. Wilbur and his mother about the "Stars and Stripes Forever." I'll do it somehow. Instinct, or maybe I've developed conditioned reflexes like one of Dr. Pavlov's dogs. And you dare deny that you use me.

FABIAN Use you?

DOLLY Constantly . . . selfishly . . . shamelessly!

FABIAN But, sweetheart, of course.

DOLLY (*Surprised*) You admit it?

FABIAN I insist on it. (*He laughs good-naturedly*) I'd use my eighty-three-year-old grandmother—or yours—if it would help me. (*Then, turning on her*) Now you think back a bit, my high-minded young harpist. Did I ever use you to fight for more money, or bigger billing? I used you to build a fine orchestra, playing great music—of my choice. For that I'm willing to use people, or abuse people; trample them, cheat them, climb over them—anything. So I'm not a nice fellow. So I won't get an award during Brotherhood Week. I am a conductor! Only the composer rates higher than that. The rest are stooges, to be used as I see fit.

DOLLY Including me.

FABIAN Especially you.

(*With which he kisses her*)

DOLLY (*Struggling*) Victor . . . stop it . . . let me go, or I'll scream.

FABIAN (*Loosening his grip*) Go on . . . scream.

DOLLY In a minute.

FABIAN (*Gallantly*) Whenever you're ready. Take your time.

DOLLY . . . Can't seem to catch my breath . . . palpitations . . .

FABIAN It's a good thing I'm a doctor.

(*He kisses her again and this time it carries all before it*)

DOLLY (*A wail*) Oh, Victor, I knew this would happen if we got married. (*Then*) You knew it, too.

FABIAN It never entered my mind. Anyway, what's worrying you . . . we've got two bedrooms.

(*They kiss again*)

DOLLY With locks. (*He starts leading her to the bedroom*) Where are you taking me? (*At the doorway*) Victor, do you think we should . . . we've been married such a short time.

FABIAN It's all right, Dolly . . . we were engaged for nearly fifteen years.

DOLLY Well, promise you won't think less of me.

FABIAN I promise.

DOLLY Do you mean it?

FABIAN I swear it.

DOLLY (*Yielding*) All right.

(*She goes, with a backward glance.* FABIAN, *left alone, picks up the wine and glasses, and is about to follow her when the buzzer is heard*)

FABIAN Damn!

(*He goes to the door and admits* RICHARD HILLIARD)

HILLIARD Good evening. Dr. Fabian? I'm Richard Hilliard.

FABIAN Richard Hi— Oh, my God!

HILLIARD You sent for me . . . you said . . .

(FABIAN *has grabbed his hand, not so much to greet him as to hold him*)

FABIAN (*Rapidly*) Dr. Hilliard! Yes, of course! Delighted to meet you, Doctor. Naturally, I was concerned about Dolly's fiancé . . . the kind of man she was going to marry . . . but just seeing you and shaking your hand is more than enough assurance . . .

(*He is maneuvering* HILLIARD *to the door*)

HILLIARD (*Indignantly*) Dr. Fabian, I've traveled four hundred thirty-seven miles to get here. (*And then* DOLLY *appears. She has changed into an extremely skimpy negligee, and the effect on* HILLIARD*—and* FABIAN, *for that matter—is overwhelming*) DOLLY!

DOLLY Richard, what are you doing here?

HILLIARD (*Pointing an indignant finger*) *He* sent for me.

DOLLY (*Incredulous*) He sent for you? (*All eyes are on* FABIAN) Oh, Victor!

FABIAN You see . . . (*He leans on something*) It was . . . (*Then he turns on* DOLLY) Damn it, Dolly, put some clothes on. Show a little respect for your fiancé!

Curtain

ACT THREE

ACT THREE

Backstage at the Civic Auditorium, Saturday night.

The reception room of the conductor's suite; a functional dressing room, shower, etc., are off this room at center stage.

It is a large room, with comfortable chairs, chaise and other furniture, decorated with framed photographs of musicians of the past and present.

At rise, CHESTER *is unpacking the contents of a large suitcase, most of the stuff already neatly laid out on the chaise and adjoining tables. An evening suit—tails, trousers, waistcoat—is on a hanger.*

DOLLY *enters from the door at left. She is wearing a bouffant evening dress and looks lovely, but she doesn't seem happy in it.*

CHESTER (*Admiringly*) Good evening, Mrs. Fabian.

DOLLY Pretty, isn't it? (*She kicks the skirt aside, moodily*) It was a Butterick pattern. Three dollars and twelve cents to make, including depreciation and overhead. (*She passes the dress suit on the hanger and draws back her fist as if to slug it*) And wait till you get the bill!

CHESTER Would you like a drink, Mrs. Fabian?

DOLLY I have had a drink, Chester. In the past three days I have also had sleeping pills, tranquillizers, Dexedrine, antibiotics, probiotics . . . (*Abruptly*) What have you got?

CHESTER A little brandy.

DOLLY Ah, brandy; that knits up the raveled sleeve of care. Well, Chester. I might have just the teeniest sip—(*He has produced a silver flask and she plucks it deftly from his hand*) Never mind the glass, Chester.

(*She takes a deep, pronounced gulp*)

CHESTER (*Anxiously*) Mrs. Fabian!

(*She holds the flask behind her, groping*)

DOLLY Damn fool designer—I told him I wanted hip pockets on this dress. (*Hands him the flask*) You keep it, Chester—but, please, stay close to me.

CHESTER My pleasure, Mrs. Fabian.

DOLLY Mrs. Fabian, Mrs. Fabian, Mrs. Fabian! That name! Ah, Chester, I wish you could have known me as a young girl—(*Pathetically*) You would have liked me. (*Darkly*) And then came Victor Fabian. Came to tune my harp, and stayed to fix my wagon. (*Again, passing the dress suit, she kicks at the tail of it*) Sneak!

CHESTER These last few days have been tense, haven't they?

DOLLY Just waking and sleeping. Poor Richard! What I've done to him!

CHESTER I saw Professor Hilliard earlier this evening . . .

DOLLY Did he—did he ask for me?

CHESTER I don't think he saw me. He was just pacing up and down in the lobby.

DOLLY The national pastime! Victor sent for him. Do you hear, Chester—*sent* for him. It was all part of a low, cunning plot. (*Swings at the suit*) Swine!

CHESTER (*Delicately*) I gather that Professor Hilliard made —well, a surprise appearance . . .

DOLLY Yes, you could gather that. (*The memory seems to be too much for her*) You know those French bedroom farces? . . . Well, there we were, and for once, good old Victor let *me* play the lead.

CHESTER Couldn't you explain?

DOLLY Oh, certainly. (*Addressing a mythical* HILLIARD) You see, Richard, Victor was taken ill suddenly. He has these fits and I'm the only one who knows where he hides the medicine. No, darling, I couldn't stop to dress—that might have been fatal. (*And looking up at* CHESTER'*s expression*) Well, you try making up a story to cover that situation . . . (*Bitterly*) And I was standing in a terrible draft!

CHESTER What did Dr. Fabian do?

DOLLY Ah, an excellent question. What did Dr. Fabian do? Dr. Fabian, his white plume of chivalry unsullied, ran for cover. "You and Richard must have a lot to say to each other," were his last words as he disappeared over the horizon. Dr. Fabian! (*Aims a swipe at the full-dress suit*)

Typhoid carrier! (*She pauses, surveys the equipment laid out by* CHESTER) Look at all that! Three complete changes, from the skin out, just to conduct one concert. You know why, don't you? (*In a secretive whisper*) He *sweats.* (CHESTER *has begun to carry the equipment into the dressing room.* DOLLY *flicks at the lapel of the hanging dress suit*) Legion of Honor! They must be taking in everybody. (*She turns away from the suit as* CHESTER *comes in for another load, and finds herself confronted by a row of framed autographed photos*) God, why do musicians spend half their lives writing illiterate lies on photographs. Listen to this one: "To my esteemed and beloved colleagues, after a memorable concert—Miklos Harvani." I'll say it was memorable. Miklos turned up reeking of slivovitz and I had to help him find his chin so he could get the violin under it. Then Victor played the introduction to the Brahms *Concerto* and good old Miklos, beaming from ear to ear, whipped right into the solo part of the Beethoven. (*A deep sigh*) Ah, Chester, there are moments when I wish with all my heart that Antonius Stradivarius had been run over when he was a little boy. (*Passing the dress suit, she again draws back as if to slug it*) Look at him! Look at that arrogant sneer!

CHESTER Want to try a little more brandy?

DOLLY No, that's the coward's way out. (*Slumps down in a chair*) Which reminds me—where is Bluebeard?

CHESTER Doing a radio interview in the control booth upstairs. A program called "Truth Today." The Voice of America is rebroadcasting it.

DOLLY And they're interviewing *him?* Well, there goes the cold war. (*She takes a cigarette, and* CHESTER *drops what he is doing to strike a match*) Thank you, Chester.

CHESTER May I say something, Mrs. Fabian?

DOLLY You may.

CHESTER Whatever your feelings, you've done a great job here for him.

(*Indicating the suit*)

DOLLY Him? Oh, him! (*Then, grimly*) He's done a great job for me, too.

CHESTER I mean it. And I know. When we were on tour, by this time—before the first concert—the natives were usually boiling tar and plucking chickens. Here—well, the way things are going, I think I know why he had such a fantastic success when you were with him before.

DOLLY (*Pleased*) Why, thank you, Chester. (*Curiously*) How do you like working for the monst—(*Hastily*) I mean "maestro"?

CHESTER I don't think you're supposed to *like* it. He takes a lot of looking-after, doesn't he?

DOLLY Oh, not much more than the average-sized aircraft carrier.

CHESTER (*Soberly*) But with it all . . . whatever it takes . . . I hope some day to hear something I've done sound like one of his really good performances. I climb up into the top gallery, or stand way in the back . . . (*Embarrassed*) Don't laugh; it gives me a religious feeling.

DOLLY Who's laughing? He is a musician, Chester. With everything horrible and wonderful the word implies. (*Looking at* CHESTER *curiously*) Are you married?

CHESTER Engaged. A girl I met in New York—at Juilliard.

DOLLY Juilliard, eh? A musician?

CHESTER She's studying the harp.

DOLLY The harp! And you're going to be a conductor? (*She grabs his hand*) Be kind to her, Chester. (*Pitifully*) Don't crush her fragile, tender spirit. When you're a famous conductor, think of me now and again, and then for my sake smile at her and say something kind.

CHESTER I promise.

DOLLY Thank you.

(*Overcome by emotion and booze, she finishes in tears. She gropes blindly for the handkerchief in the pocket of* FABIAN'S *suit, uses it to the fullest extent, then puts it back*)

CHESTER (*Anxiously*) Mrs. Fabian, would you like to lie down? . . . Stretch out quietly for a few minutes?

DOLLY None of your conductor tricks, Chester.

(*Then* ARCHER *enters at left, in a dinner jacket, wearing a black, broad-brimmed hat which is his impresario badge*)

ARCHER Dolly! (*Admiringly*) This is how teachers are dressing nowadays?

DOLLY I like to be a credit to the profession.

ARCHER You are, you are. Well, how does it feel, Dolly? This same old room . . . the auditorium . . . just before a concert? . . .

DOLLY Mixed emotions, I guess. How did Lizzie Borden feel when she came back to Fall River?

ARCHER (*Reproachfully*) Dolly! (*Then*) Chester—where's the radio? We can hear Fabian. He is being interviewed— (*While* CHESTER *is getting it*) I only hope he's careful. Nowadays, an interview on radio or television, the questions they ask. I went on such a program once. Some fellow named Grollis or Hollis—or something like that. My God! The man says good evening and in the same breath he wants to know: am I queer . . . did I ever manage a Communist . . . and who was sleeping with the prima ballerina in my ballet company? Go tell him, it was her brother. (CHESTER *has found the radio, turns it on, and goes back to the dressing room*)

ANNOUNCER'S VOICE And on this last tour, Dr. Fabian, you had extensive guest engagements, no doubt?

FABIAN'S VOICE Here and abroad, yes, quite a few. Twenty

appearances with major symphony orchestras and a gala performance of *Swan Lake* at the Bolshoi Theatre in Moscow.

ARCHER One rehearsal and he had them wishing Stalin was back.

ANNOUNCER'S VOICE The Civic Symphony here is often referred to as your creation, Dr. Fabian. Would you care to comment on that?

DOLLY *I* would.

FABIAN'S VOICE If it is, I hope I am worthy of it.

DOLLY Oh, God!

FABIAN'S VOICE To me this is not merely an auditorium, it is a shrine. And on the stage below, that is not just a music stand—

DOLLY (*Quickly*) It is an altar.

FABIAN'S VOICE It is an altar. (*She glows with pride at having outguessed the maestro, who continues pouring on the syrup*) What do we mean when we say "conductor"? The accepted definition is "leader" but I think of myself only as a guide . . . an humble pilgrim to the great golden gate of music.

DOLLY I demand equal time to answer that.

ANNOUNCER'S VOICE In the past, as I recall, you did not always see eye to eye artistically with the orchestra trustees—

(ARCHER *switches off the radio*)

ARCHER That part I know already. (*With a sigh*) You see how sweet and reasonable he has become, Dolly? A different person entirely.

DOLLY I'm glad. Your cousin—the Mexican lawyer—Pancho Archer?

ARCHER Don Felipe. What about him?

DOLLY Call him. Tell him I'm on my way.

ARCHER (*Pained*) So soon?

DOLLY Tonight. (*As he is about to protest*) We made a bargain, Max. After the concert, Saturday night—remember?

ARCHER Of course. You're really going, Dolly—tonight?

DOLLY Surprised?

ARCHER Well, I was hoping. You know, proximity is nine-tenths of the law. You and Victor . . . under one roof . . .

DOLLY That was a *grand* idea!

ARCHER It could have been. The only thing—on your wedding night—what a time for your fiancé to show up!

DOLLY It certainly made my week! And who arranged that bit of split-second timing?

ARCHER So he did it? But he didn't know how it would turn out.

DOLLY Ha!

ARCHER Besides, he was desperate. You should be flattered. It shows how much he loves you.

DOLLY You mean, if he didn't love me, he wouldn't louse up my life?

ARCHER And he needs you, Dolly.

DOLLY Victor needs Victor. And they deserve each other. Go on, Max—call Don José—

ARCHER (*Mechanically*) Don Felipe. All right. (*He starts out at left*) Tonight! Is there a plane tonight?

DOLLY At midnight, for Tulsa. Change there for Acapulco.

ARCHER Tulsa? In the middle of the night—*Tulsa?* You want a divorce that much?

(*He goes out, sadly shaking his head.* DOLLY, *left alone, picks up the radio, turns it on*)

FABIAN'S VOICE —as you know, my tour was not concluded when I accepted this engagement. Following triumphs abroad, I induced my manager to accept engagements in Sioux City, Iowa, and other Midwestern cultural centers. But there was a second, more intimate factor in my decision to return—continuation of my tour meant separation from my wife. (*As* DOLLY *stares wide-eyed at the set*) Believing as I do in the simple American creed—togetherness—

DOLLY Oh! (*She snaps off the radio with so much vehemence that the knob comes off in her hand. She draws back, as if to hurl this to stage left when the door opens on that side, and* RICHARD HILLIARD *makes one of those ill-timed entrances for which he is becoming famous.* HILLIARD, *a youngish chap, seems to have aged mysteriously after only three days with a symphony orchestra*) Richard!

HILLIARD Yes, Dolly.

DOLLY A drink, Richard?

HILLIARD No, thank you.

DOLLY What've you been doing?

HILLIARD Thinking.

DOLLY Oh. (*Hopefully*) Something nuclear?

HILLIARD No. (*He looks at* DOLLY *steadily for a moment. His is a keen, analytical gaze*) Are you in love with Victor Fabian?

(*The shock of the question seems to give* DOLLY *some internal upheaval*)

DOLLY Richard! You've been drinking.

HILLIARD Answer my question, Dolly.

DOLLY All right. No, I do not love Victor Fabian. Victor Fabian is a dangerous lunatic and I wouldn't go within fifty yards of him unless he were muzzled and chained.

HILLIARD Do you mean that, Dolly?

DOLLY I'm leaving for Mexico—tonight—to divorce him. I won't even use his name. I'm asking the court to give me back my maiden name—(*Proudly*) Dorothea Snodgrass!

HILLIARD Then the other night . . . didn't mean what I thought it meant? . . .

DOLLY I told you—he put something in my drink.

HILLIARD (*Warmly*) Dolly!

(*He opens his arms wide. She stares at him. It is suddenly too much of a good thing*)

DOLLY Richard, I'm staying in Mexico.

(*His arms are still spread wide—he* is *absent-minded*)

HILLIARD I'll join you there.

DOLLY (*Firmly, kindly*) No, Richard.

HILLIARD But it works out perfectly. The University of Mexico has been after me to lecture there on heat particles.

DOLLY No, Richard.

HILLIARD It doesn't have to be heat particles. I'll do expanding gases.

DOLLY No, Richard.

HILLIARD Oh! (*He examines each of his arms, and identifying them as his own he lowers them*) I see.

DOLLY No, you don't. Nobody does. Not even me. I'm sorry, Richard.

HILLIARD So am I. I'll miss you, Dolly. (*Crosses to the door*) When I was young, I studied piano. I'm sorry now that I didn't practice.

(*He goes out. After a moment* ARCHER *enters*)

ARCHER What happened to the president—he looks crushed.

DOLLY You ought to know—you helped with the crushing.

(FABIAN *enters. He is wearing a sweater and odd trousers; has a lot of changing to do*)

FABIAN Max tells me you're going to Mexico—tonight? Why?

DOLLY Why does anyone go to Mexico? For guitar lessons.

ARCHER Victor, look at the time—the concert—you're not dressed.

DOLLY We made a bargain, Victor, and while you may have had other plans, I'm keeping it.

FABIAN Dolly, I swear to you—when Hilliard turned up the other night, it was a complete surprise to me—

DOLLY Stop it! If you say another word about that, or about anything, I'll scream.

FABIAN I did send for him. I admit it, and I know it was a dirty—

(DOLLY *screams. She cuts loose with a high B-flat, or thereabouts, that shakes the rafters*)

ARCHER My God, stop, Dolly—you'll bring fire engines.

DOLLY A sample of the work that can be done on this machine. (*Ominously*) I am very nearly at the breaking point. And I promise you, if I break, this will be a concert to remember.

ARCHER Victor, please—hurry up—don't worry about Dolly. (*He is pushing him to the dressing room*) I will entertain her. Eh, Dolly?

(*And he closes the door, turning to* DOLLY)

DOLLY Go on, Max—entertain me.

ARCHER I called my cousin—Don Felipe— It is all arranged.

DOLLY (*Reluctantly*) Well, I like the sound of that—

ARCHER Only first you must discuss with Victor the question of a property settlement, and alimony.

DOLLY Alimony? You mean, take money from him?

ARCHER If not, how will you live?

DOLLY I'll hold up gas stations. Anything!

(*The door flies open, revealing* FABIAN *in black shoes and silk hose, shorts and very little else*)

FABIAN Dolly, try to understand. I know that what I did was detestable . . .

DOLLY I do understand, Victor, and I detest you.

FABIAN But I did it for us—

DOLLY Us?
(She is rocked for a moment, then cuts loose with another scream)

FABIAN *(Hastily, in flight)* Max, give her something.

ARCHER *(Timidly)* You want something, Dolly?

DOLLY His head—on a platter.

ARCHER When you told him you wanted a divorce—there was another man—honestly, Dolly, he went out of his mind. Not about this engagement, or a contract, or anything like that. Just the idea of losing you to this professor. He was like a wild man.

DOLLY He was born that way. *(The dressing room door flies open and* FABIAN *appears again, this time having added a shirt to his ensemble, wing collar, and a white tie, the latter dangling loose)* God, what hideous knees!

FABIAN *(Instantly)* They are awful, aren't they? Max, remind me Monday to have them broken and reset. *(He approaches* DOLLY, *ingratiatingly dangling the loose end of his tie)* Dolly—for luck—the way you used to, before a concert . . . ? (*At the look in her eye, hastily*) Don't scream—I'll go quietly.

DOLLY Come here. (*He looks doubtful*) Come *here.* (*He moves within range, and she reaches for the ends of the tie*) I wish I knew how to make a hangman's knot.

FABIAN Maybe if you broke an album of records over my head—

DOLLY Shut up!

FABIAN Yes, Dolly.

(*She works on the tie in silence for a moment*)

DOLLY And keep your Adam's apple from bobbing up and down.

FABIAN (*Humbly*) It's trying to tell you something.

DOLLY I won't listen. (*She finishes the tie with a vicious twist*) There!

FABIAN Thank you, Dolly. (*He goes back to the dressing room, climbs into his pants in the open doorway, then puts on his waistcoat, being fully dressed except for the tail coat*) Did Max tell you the good news, Dolly? I've accepted an offer to do the Beethoven *Ninth Symphony* with the A Capella Chorus and Orchestra of Acapulco, Mexico—

DOLLY (*Wailing*) No-o-o-o!

FABIAN "Whither thou goest, I goest. Thy people shall be my people."

DOLLY (*Fiercely*) It's a lie. You made it up. There is no Acapulco Chorus in A Capella, Mexico. There can't be.

FABIAN There will be.

(DOLLY, *at a loss, plants her feet apart and screams.* CHESTER *comes in on this*)

CHESTER Is something wrong?

FABIAN Mrs. Fabian is screaming. (*She stops abruptly*) Ah, the all clear . . .

DOLLY Chester . . . my friend . . .

(MR. WILBUR, *also in a dinner jacket, looms up in the open doorway at left*)

WILBUR 'Evening. Can I come in?

ARCHER Of course. What an honor! I didn't think you would come to the concert *personally*.

FABIAN We thought you might drop in for intermission.

WILBUR I hemmed and I hawed and then I said, Shucks, it's the Centennial and I guess once every hundred years I can stand it. (*To* DOLLY) My, what a pretty dress.

DOLLY Thank you, Mr. Wilbur.

WILBUR Mother certainly enjoyed your visit, Mrs. Fabian. She asked me particularly to tell you.

DOLLY Thank you.

(*She curtsies, has a little trouble rising from it, but she makes it.* WILBUR *has cleared a space on a table and takes a bulky legal-looking document from his pocket*)

FABIAN What's that document, Mr. Wilbur?

WILBUR Oh—hasn't Mrs. Fabian told you?

FABIAN Mrs. Fabian tells me so much that sometimes I lose track.

WILBUR Oh, you'd remember this—it's the contract.

ARCHER (*He has picked it up*) For next season!

WILBUR For three seasons. You see, Mrs. Fabian had some nice long talks with Mother, and Mother talked to me, and I talked to the trustees—

(DOLLY *and* FABIAN *are staring at each other; she shifts her gaze uncertainly*)

DOLLY What's the big federal case? Didn't any of you ever see a contract before?

ARCHER Beautiful . . . (*He is leafing through it hurriedly*) Poetry . . . violins on a distant shore . . .

FABIAN (*Deliberately*) Mr. Wilbur, does Mother know that Mrs. Fabian is leaving for Mexico?

(ARCHER *groans*)

WILBUR Mexico? No, you didn't mention it, did you, Mrs. Fabian?

DOLLY I couldn't . . . (*With a helpless shrug*) I'm a wetback.

ARCHER No, no. She's only going for a few days—to buy pre-Columbian dogs.

FABIAN She's staying in Mexico—to divorce me. (*At this* ARCHER *makes a sound like escaping steam*) That's right, isn't it, Dolly? (DOLLY *turns away*) So Mother ought to know that all she's getting for three years is my lovable self.

WILBUR That's different, isn't it? (*Plucks the contract from* ARCHER's *lifeless fingers*) Mother doesn't like to buy a pig in a poke . . . but I'll tell her—

DOLLY Victor Fabian, you are the most treacherous, underhanded man I have ever known. You put in a lifetime of lying, swindling and assorted double-dealing, and now you're bristling with moral fiber—only to irritate me. Well, that's not your contract—it's mine. I drank tea till it ran out of my pores and sang your praises till I got polyps on my vocal cords. Well, hear this: You're not turning decent at my expense. You'll sign the contract and I'm staying right here to see that you work out every clause. (*He looks at her blankly for a moment*) And you call yourself a conductor? Damn it, Victor, I'm a harpist.

(*That does it. They are in an instant clinch.* WILBUR *looks at them, fascinated.* ARCHER, *meanwhile, plucks the contract back from* WILBUR, *spreads it invitingly, pulls up a chair and whisks out a fountain pen.* DOLLY *and* FABIAN *are still playing "living statues"*)

ARCHER Here, Mr. Wilbur, take my pen. It was a gift from the late Czar, the same pen he used to free the serfs.

WILBUR (*Doubtfully*) A Papermate?

(WILBUR *is watching* DOLLY *and* FABIAN, *still frozen in Position A.* ARCHER *tugs at his sleeve reassuringly*)

ARCHER It's all right—they could be hours.

WILBUR Are they all right?

ARCHER We should all be in the same condition.

(*He is relieved, nevertheless, as is* WILBUR, *when the lovers break apart*)

FABIAN Dolly, I'm so glad.

DOLLY So am I.

FABIAN I'll whip through the first half and you meet me here during intermission—

DOLLY Victor! (*Nudging him*) Mr. Wilbur—

FABIAN Oh, yes.

(WILBUR *indicates the contract laid out, and extends the pen.*

WILBUR After you, my dear doctor.

FABIAN Thank you. (*He sits down, takes the pen*) You've looked at this, Max?

ARCHER It's beautiful. Sign, Victor.

(WILBUR stands by, and idly starts whistling the "trio" from the "Stars and Stripes Forever." FABIAN is just about to sign when he becomes aware of it. He looks up)

FABIAN What's that you're whistling, Mr. Wilbur?

WILBUR Whistling? Was I whistling?

ARCHER (*Desperately*) It was the *William Tell* "Overture."

FABIAN We understand each other about the "Stars and Stripes Forever," don't we, Mr. Wilbur?

WILBUR (*Beaming*) Perfectly. Mother was in the wrong, and she said so. That's Mother. Mrs. Fabian made it all clear and Mother was delighted. After all, for this concert, your program was all arranged—

FABIAN What do you mean, *this* concert?

WILBUR You're playing it next week, of course.

FABIAN (*Sweetly*) Am I? (*Puts down pen, folds his arms deliberately*) Mrs. Fabian made that clear, did she? (*Turns on* DOLLY, *romance forgotten*) You two-bit Machiavelli, how dare you?

DOLLY Forgive me. I was so much in love I forgot you were impossible. Victor, don't you realize what this means?

ARCHER It's such a little march. You wouldn't even have to rehearse it—the orchestra knows it by heart.

FABIAN My compliments to Mother, Mr. Wilbur—(*He is about to hand back the contract*)

DOLLY No! I won't let you. (*She puts herself between* WILBUR *and* FABIAN) Victor, please. Not for Mr. Wilbur's mother, for me. Call it a wedding present—anything. Just once for me—be reasonable.

FABIAN No! (*He moves her aside gently, facing* WILBUR) I want very much to please Mother, Mr. Wilbur.

WILBUR I'll tell her—but Mother believes in deeds, not words. (*To the others, proudly*) Mother has a head on her shoulders.

ARCHER (*Instantly, stoutly*) Absolutely! I've seen it.

FABIAN Mother can have the "Stars and Stripes Forever," Mr. Wilbur. I'll stand under her window and sing it, every night—come rain or come shine. Mother can have anything. All I ask is these two hours a week, Saturday night, from eight-thirty to half-past ten, for my concert, and if you give me just that much, for the remaining one hundred and sixty-six hours a week I will belong to Mother, body and soul. She can tell me what to eat, what to wear, what to think and how to vote. Tell Mother that, and tell her I mean it with all my heart—(*Then forcibly*) But tell your dear saintly white-haired mother this—if she dares to lay a finger on my music I'll kick her teeth in. (*To* ARCHER) Max, is that clear?

ARCHER (*Respectfully*) Certainly, Doctor.

FABIAN Dolly?

DOLLY Yes, Victor.

(*The process of tuning has stopped offstage, and the room, too, is hushed.* FABIAN *throws the contract on the table*)

FABIAN (*To* WILBUR) So now we understand each other.

(*A knock at the door*)

CHESTER (*Off*) Ready for you, Dr. Fabian.

FABIAN Coming. (*To* WILBUR, *crisply*) Sit down. (WILBUR *sits down, abruptly*) Max, your pen. (ARCHER *hands it to him, he hands it to* WILBUR) Sign. (*He turns away without even waiting to see if it works, but it does*) Dolly, my coat.

DOLLY (*Humbly*) Yes, Doctor.

(*She gets the tail coat, holds it for him as he slips into it.* CHESTER *is already holding the door open and there is a blaze of reflected light outside the door from the auditorium and stage lighting.* FABIAN *pauses in the open doorway, his eyes closed for a moment, as if preparing himself, then strides out. After a slight pause, there is a mounting burst of applause.* DOLLY *sinks into a chair. The applause continues, as in a real ovation, then starts to subside*)

WILBUR Listen to them! My, your husband is popular, Mrs. Fabian!

DOLLY He must be. I finally got to like him myself!! (*Then two taps of* FABIAN'S *offstage baton, followed by, of all things, the "Stars and Stripes Forever." It blares out big and loud and brassy*) Listen, Mr. Wilbur— *Listen!*

ARCHER (*Reverently*) The "Stars and Stripes Forever." (*He holds his hat over his heart*) My God! He's being reasonable.

(*He seems dazed by this final upheaval*)

WILBUR I hope Mother is wearing her hearing aid. (*He moves to* DOLLY, *who is in the open doorway*) Mrs. Fabian . . . can you see?

DOLLY Yes . . . wait—(*Gesturing for silence*) Yes, I think so . . . they are! (*And as the march swings into the main theme*) Yes, they are! My God, the piccolo players are standing up!

Curtain